# UTAH'S SPECIAL BLEND

# UTAH'S SPECIAL BLEND

## *Local Humorists Spill the Beans...*

*Compiled by*

*Steve Odenthal*

# Copyright

# Dedication

Collecting stories for a book of humor during a pandemic is a daunting task. Still, that work is nothing when compared to the load for those who put one foot in front of the other each day and carry on after the loss of a loved one to the silent assassin among us.

This book is dedicated to the families that struggle and deal with their very personal voids each day. Our writers hope that some brief laughter will help a bit with aching hearts. We share in your losses with our own. Be safe.

# Table of Contents

# Foreword

The book you are holding is very funny. It was designed to be just that—a book of humor to serve as an escape pod for the reader. But it is not written at an amusing moment in history. The year 2020 will be long remembered for its challenges and tragic death-tolls. If ever there were a year that required a strong cup of coffee, it would be 2020; yes, even in Utah, a unique brew might be just what the doctor ordered to get us through.

*Utah's Special Blend* is a collection of short humor contributed by some excellent writers with a strong Utah background. Whether you believe you know the state or not, I think you will come away after reading, having learned a little something unexpected. I did not give a specific topic to the contributors, as I trusted their instincts, and I believe they came through with flying colors. In each case, the authors use their comedic voice to relate a slice of life to you hoping that your day will be brighter. I'm sure you will find a new author to follow in these pages. Remember to smile and laugh even in the hard times—laughter is the sound we most remember with our hearts.

# Cold Water Canyon Flood of '83

## *Steve Odenthal*

One of the benefits of living in Utah is its unique scenery. The land is famous for its red rocks and arches down south, but we in the northern part of the state do not want when it comes to beautiful views. Most of the population lives in the north half of Utah, where the Wasatch mountain range looms large, stretching from Brigham City to Nephi, and alternates between the exposed rock face and massive wooded green areas full of wildlife. Those who came before in days of old to settle this place were wise to build their cities right at the base of these picturesque mountains. And the desire to snuggle up to these bedrock and granite wonders still exists today, as each new housing tract strings new mini-mansions across the benches, with each home built to capture the best view of either valley floor or the majestic peaks.

A benefit of this proximity to wildlife and nature is that within minutes you can hike to, explore, and get thoroughly lost in that scenery. When friends from out of state come to visit, they always comment on how fast our little hike turned from beautiful and serene to dangerous with me as a guide. Typically, after the search and rescue squad has found us clinging to one of those granite faces, and hypothermia is no longer a concern, my visitors (most former friends by this time) comment on how breathtaking the views are from so high up there and how very fast the helicopters responded to our situation.

Usually, my guests don't spend the night as the day hike has made them somewhat nervous, and the idea of a hotel room in a larger city seems less like roughing it and more calming to them. It is too bad when they choose that route because I never get the chance to tell them exaggerated tales of our wildlife and the occasional Sasquatch that meander through now and again. Still, it is their loss as I could have quickly taken them to Coldwater Creek, which wound its way to the valley floor, not eighty feet past my back fence. I would have done it, too, had I been aware that they didn't want the excitement of a more significant excursion.

Coldwater Creek ran between housing tracts in North Ogden at the time and proved itself a babbling water park for the neighborhood kids. It flowed out of the mountains through Coldwater Canyon, which now boasts a proudly hung, free-flying, huge American flag called "The Major." It is a tremendously patriotic sight that brings a tear to my eye each time I see it. But "The Major" was not flying back in 1983 when I lived there. The well-forested Coldwater Canyon stood over and provided an active flood plain for the city's dwellings below. Dependent upon the water-year experienced and the naturally occurring run-off, Coldwater Canyon could have an average amount of water running through it and into our babbling kid-friendly creek. It could also have a large and dangerous amount of liquid and tree limbs, causing havoc and flooding during a bad year. But 1983 was to be neither of those type of years—the locals anticipated a Godzilla year. Not just tree limbs were expected, but tree trunks, Volkswagon-sized pieces of granite, and seventy-foot pines would be floating, and smashing, and crushing, and doing, you know, usual Godzilla flood sorta things. Beautiful or not, nestled below Coldwater Canyon was not the place to be in June of 1983.

The city mobilized, as you do in an emergency, but this was a time long ago when cell phones were just starting to hit the U.S. market. There were not many, if any, in North Ogden, Utah, so radio-dispatched crews from the city took to their stations each day, spacing themselves a football field apart so they could tell when the upper creek would breach, and all heck would break loose. The top station would radio down to the next station, and that position would pass the word on his walkie-talkie until someone would fix things or at least get the info out to residents. In fairness, with the passing of years, I may have lost a few details and the strategy involved in the city's plan, but I do remember when the workday ended, North

Ogden residents were called upon to spell the city workers through the night. That is one thing you can count on in Utah—entire communities rally to a cause in a heartbeat when serious events occur.

The organization here is impressive to witness, and for this imminent danger, contact lists and phone trees were already in use. City folk dutifully answered the call to replace the warning monitors stretching from the city up through the canyon in 4-hour shifts after the city workers left for the day. As luck would have it, my assigned shift was to be at the top-most monitor station at 4:00 A.M. Yes, that is four o'clock in the morning, which seemed a dark and undesirable time to be hiking into a wooded canyon. The assignment call came early in the evening, no doubt, to allow some time to sleep a bit before starting the task. But, being a relative newcomer to North Ogden, I wasn't quite sure of how to hike up to Coldwater Canyon. I immediately called some of the old heads in the area that I knew to verify where to go to fulfill my civic duty. Many of those longer-termed residents were helpful, with some even anxious to tell me where to go.

***

Call number one went something like this:

"Hey, Paul. This is Steve. I guess I'm pulling the 4 A.M. shift up on the mountain. Any idea how I get to station one?"

"Wow. They are throwing you right in, aren't they?"

"Well, we all need to do our duty."

"There's that. But you haven't been here long enough to see a Godzilla year. They used to put the seasoned guys in station one. Might be going for expendables this time around. You'll be in the thick of it."

"The thick of what? They told me I'd just be a watchman. I'd just radio down if things started flooding."

"Technically, that'd be true. Keep that walkie talkie on. Oh, and stay leaned back on a pine or a boulder, real secure, like."

"Why... why is that?"

"It will be easier to find ya, should the worst happen."

"Believe me. I'll radio down and be out of there if things break loose. Don't worry about me."

"Oh, then you've out-run a flood before. I didn't know…"

"Not yet, but I am big on self-preservation. If the flood starts, I'll get down to the flatlands."

"One way or another, you definitely will. Been to station one, before?"

"No, that's why I called. I know I keep going north of 1700 N on Mountain Road, but don't know where the cut-up is."

"Just get out of the car and start hiking on Sasquatch Trail. You'll see the tire ruts."

"Sasquatch Trail?"

"Yeah, the city calls it something else on the Master Plan. They want to play down the sightings. They discourage much use of the trail."

"The city?"

"No, the Sasquatch."

"Right, the Yeti."

"Don't drive your Jeep. They really don't like Jeeps. Flip 'em like hotcakes. That's why you'll want to hike up. Doesn't rile 'em up as bad."

***

Most of the other calls that evening went along the same line. None built a high degree of confidence in my survival in a Godzilla flood year. Some maniacal laughter dotted a few of the conversations, mostly when my assignment to station one was made known. I repeatedly heard that station one was indeed where the action was and also that Jeeps were discouraged. The outpost was closest to the creekbed at its most vulnerable breach point and covered in dense sagebrush and undergrowth, but quite a beautiful spot during the day, the old-timers explained. However, at 4 A.M., it was highly unlikely that I would be able to see my hand in front of my face, let alone a Sasquatch paw.

Having heard more than enough, I turned in for the short night. After a not-so-restful sleep, I found myself eye-to-eye with an obsessed alarm clock at a time that can only be described as **3:45 IN**

**THE MORNING!** Reasonable people and entire nations slumbered at that time of day, but *reasonable* people only dealt with Godzilla via black-and-white reruns on the classic sci-fi channel. This was personal. I donned my most tree-limb and boulder resistant attire and set out for Coldwater Canyon. As I pulled my Plymouth Volare off Mountain Road a bit south of Sasquatch Trail; the only place I could park was, wouldn't you know it, right next to a Jeep Cherokee. I thought about hotcakes. But there was nothing else to do but hope that Yeti spatulas were selective.

There were a lot of vehicles parked along the road. Those twenty-four stations that the new shift was relieving would clear out some of them, but our newly arriving vehicles would just replace the crowd of cars within a few minutes. I reported to the sign-in tailgate (in the mountains, you don't have desks) bathed in the spotlight of two KC lamps illuminating HQ. I told them I was replacing station one. The old head with the paperwork and a beef jerky stick rolling from side to side of his mouth like an Eastwood cigar blinked an unbroken stare at me and queried an accomplice behind him.

"Kotter, we doing expendables at station one this year?"

"Nah, Mayor says too much liability. City Attorney has a fit." Came the reply.

"We're putting you at number three." The honcho tore off a piece of paper and handed it to me.

"Is this my map?" I asked.

"No. It just says station 3. Don't need a map. Just keep going uphill till you get to number 3. Looks like you'll be relieving Jonesy. Make sure when you come up on him you make some noise, so he hears you coming. He gets edgier every year."

"Jonesy, right. I probably don't need this paper." I tried to hand it back to the boss guy.

"No. You keep it. Even better if you can pin it to your shirt. You know about putting your back to a tree or big rock, right?"

"Yeah, I've heard that."

"Great. Well, move on out then. You bring a side-arm?"

"Should I have?

"Well, not officially. Nevermind. Okay, we'll see you."

He pointed up the mountain, and I started my ascent of Sasquatch Trail. As I passed each station along the way, I recognized some citizens that I had seen around the city. In their daylight lit routines, I had never noticed any of them displaying the facial tics and squints displayed when my flashlight found them in the dark. A few of the stations seemed to be un-manned. But in those cases, there rose an eerie laugh or noise after I was uphill and midway to the next station. Just some of the boys having some fun, I thought. But I also silently wondered what a Sasquatch sounded like; I didn't believe that Yetis were known to laugh much. *So, yeah—probably just some of the boys, having fun.*

By the time I made it past station four, I was puffing like a freight train—Jonesy would have no problem hearing me approaching on this night. Before I could catch my breath from the moonlight exertion, a hand came to rest on my shoulder from the uphill side. I froze. It was a big hand, but I reasoned, not the size of a paw by Sasquatch standards. But even so, my flashlight hand was not obeying my brain and refused to swing upward toward the face of what I hoped was an incredibly tall Jonesy. I felt a blast of hot air by my right ear while a grotesque moan or growl filled the air around me. Suddenly, a dank stench filled my nostrils and momentarily possessed my being. I recoiled a step back, but the hairy paw was not letting its prey loose this night. Although I struggled, a barely visible outline of a gigantic form took shape and pulled me in tight.

"Worst jerky Kotter has ever brought." The voice whispered in my ear and then belched once again.

"Jonesy?" I gasped.

"Shhhh! You, my relief-man?

"I am," I admitted. "Has it been pretty quiet so far?"

"Does *that* sound real quiet to you?" He asked.

Between my panting and my heart pounding in my chest, I hadn't clued in on the rising noise of the unseen creek somewhere off to my left beyond the growth and vegetation. It was loud, not quite the roar of an ocean, but there was the unmistakable sound of rushing water or perhaps even a waterfall in the distance.

"Yeah, I hear it now." I nodded, just as a crashing boulder bounded downstream. I jumped and yelled, grasping at the walkie-talkie clipped to his belt, which had become illuminated by my flashlight as I flailed about in terror.

"We better let 'em know it's coming! Use the radio!" I pretty much screamed.

"First tour of duty, I'm guessing, right?"

"What? …Yeah." I stammered. "Is that what it sounds like? When it breaks loose?"

"Nah, that's just some rock, maybe a good-sized limb. Happens all the time up here. You'll know when the creek jumps out." Jonesy opined.

"A lot more noise, I guess?"

"Well, yeah. But, there are other ways to tell. You know those moving sidewalks they got in airports?"

"Yeah. What do moving sidewalks have to do with this?"

"Well, most of the ground you are standing on is gonna start sliding like that."

"I won't know before that? Won't the top two stations get on the radio and give us a warning?"

"That *could* happen, I suppose, but when it starts, those guys are going to be pretty busy riding it out. But if you do see either of them wash by, you *should* shout out over the talkie."

With that, Jonesy gave me a friendly but heavy-handed slap on the arm and wished me good luck.

"Well, I'm out of here." He picked up a field pack and slung it across his shoulder. "You got your flashlight, check. And a pistol? No. Well, just keep swinging your flashlight across that brush area to your right, like this from time to time." He swung his own beam toward the brush. Twelve eyeballs illuminated for a moment as his light arced uphill. "Yeah, the critters don't want any part of the creek right now. You can keep em at bay with your light now and then."

Jonesy handed me the walkie-talkie and took a step down the hill. The tall man looked back. "You good?" He asked and lit my face with his torch. My response was a little hesitant, but still, I had to ask.

"Oh, sure… I'm… good. Say, no reason to think any of those eyeballs were a Sasquatch, is there?"

7

"No way. They are too packed together. Might be a couple does, a buck or two, maybe a moose, but Sasquatch, no. They always come at you from your uphill side." He reached out and handed me a sack. "Here, keep this with you; the critters won't come near you if you munch on these." He belched again as he handed over the remaining jerky. "I may have to kill Kotter if he brings a batch like that again." He shouted over his shoulder as he trotted down and out of sight.

In the next few hours, I got a chance to reflect on my life quite a bit while eating a ton of lousy jerky. I finished my assignment without incident, at least reportable incident. I will say that with critters on my right, potential Sasquatch roaming on my uphill side, and a noisy, threatening wannabe fresh-water tsunami to my left, I never even considered nodding off. When the city emergency worker replaced me at eight A.M., I thanked him profusely and made record time getting down that canyon and back to the safety of my car. I'm sure that it was pure coincidence, but as I arrived at my vehicle, a tow truck was hauling away the Jeep Cherokee that had parked in front of me. And I'm never going to ask…

As luck would have it, the Godzilla year turned out to be relatively calm. There were some flooding spots and debris in our neighborhoods, but the damage paled compared to the State Street flood of that same year in Salt Lake City. We've always caught fish in our babbling Coldwater Creek, but Salt Lakers had never fished State Street before. It was indeed a strange year. In Utah, it is wise to remember that as scenic as it is, in flood years, there *will* be sticks.

# Hot Yoga—A Review

## *Monique Berish*

I've been doing yoga for more than twenty years. Started way back in high school. Back when yoga was, yanno, deep stretching and meditation—real yoga. I was excited to get back into it after moving to Salt Lake City. What can be a better add to my self-care routine than an hour of focusing on breathing, core, and relaxation—especially after working 12-hour shifts at the hospital. I started searching out local options. A friend offered me a free pass to "THE BEST HOT YOGA in Salt Lake City." And she was as all-caps enthusiastic about it as the advertisement. I agreed and set up a time to meet her at the studio inside Thanksgiving Point.

I should stop here and mention that although I've been doing yoga for decades and started out going to studios in my 20's when spandex was my friend, after three kids and 20 more years, I now reserve it for my living room with a purchased DVD. …Because I don't want to create a public stampede of people running from the studio when I flowed from plank position to downward dog. So this would be my first studio experience in decades.

Another important, little factoid about me: I do NOT like the heat. I lived in Arizona for exactly ten months. The reason why I lived in Arizona for ten months was because I could not handle living there for eleven. I get whiny, cranky, and, in general, become a person no one wants to be around. So for me to consider hot yoga meant that I: A. really trusted this friend and B. was not in a sound decision-making place.

On the day of our little outing, I was nervous, but I thought I was being silly. *It's yoga. You're really good at yoga. What's the worst that could happen?* I'm not sure why I dared the universe like that, but in true Murphy style, the universe wholeheartedly accepted the challenge.

We walked in, and immediately I felt like a fish out of water. The reception area was stark white and very minimalist yet still posh. At the front desk a man in his 20's with the obligatory hipster beard grunted when my friend handed him our free passes. Everything in the room was environmentally focused. There were racks of an eco-friendly hemp clothing line, a reusable water jugs display, and biodegradable water cups at the water cooler. Each with signs detailing the atrocities your current garb was creating for the environment. If that didn't give you enough to feel inadequate about, taking up the entire wall was a sign asking for patrons to donate to save the endangered animals. I could almost feel the slap of judgment when I walked past it without putting money in the collection box. I'm a nurse. Endangered animals aren't my passion. What can I say? I'm a monster.

We went to the locker room to put up our valuables. It was at this point my friend pulled out her water bottle. It looked like she was planning a backpacking expedition into the desert, not a one-hour yoga session. This thing was a 64 oz. growler of insulated, frosty refreshment. I pulled out my 16 oz. bottled water and half expected to hear a gasp from the women in the room at my audacity to bring a plastic, disposable bottle into this sanctuary for the woke. No gasp erupted, but when I left the locker room, I did get a dirty look from the bearded hipster who made it a point to mention that plastic water bottles were not allowed, but since I was a guest, he would make an exception. I apologized for my entire generation's lack of environmental awareness and proceeded toward the studio.

We stood in a vestibule area that had glass walls allowing you to see into the studio. An air conditioner blasted above us, and there was a bench on one side along with a door that led into the room. I approached the window wall and studied the scene where I was about to commit public yoga. The actual room was nothing much to look at. The few studios I'd seen in the past were somewhat smallish, dark places with a lot of Eastern decorations and fancy lighting. The general snootiness of this place made me assume that this would be over the top extravagant. Instead, I was about to enter a plain, vast dance studio with a 1980's drop ceiling and an entire wall of picture windows that looked out to a cement wall in the parking lot. Well, at least they won't be able to make it too hot in here with a space this large, I thought. Just then, my friend leaned in and whispered, "This place is the best because it has the hottest hot yoga."

"How hot is it?"

"About 109 degrees."

It was at that moment I seriously considered backing out.

"Wait. What? 109 degrees!"

"It'll be fine. You'll love it. It helps with the stretching."

"I'm sure I'll be very flexible and stretchy when I pass out on the floor."

"It's really not that bad. Trust me! You're gonna love it!"

The door to the studio opened, and a lady, dripping in sweat, entered the vestibule where we lingered waiting for the instructor to appear. The gust of heat hit me, and I thought my face was going to melt off. Even the blasting air conditioner above us was no match for the furnace we would be entering. At those temperatures I wouldn't be feeling limber; I'd be feeling medium-rare. There was a surprising amount of people inside the room for a weekday afternoon class. Everyone was already sweating. I was baffled about why they wanted to expose themselves to the heat any longer than necessary. The instructor entered and we followed after him. I realized quickly that they were there, enduring the heat because they wanted the best spot...next to the door that blasted the air conditioning. I claimed a small spot on the wood floor right at the front and, facing the floor to ceiling mirrors, and began to stretch.

The instructor started off slow, which was good, but then began calling out names of moves I'd never heard of. If that wasn't bad enough, he gave minimal instruction on how to get into those poses assuming all in the class were those that paid the monthly dues and not us peasants with one-time, free passes. I was left to look to my neighbor for guidance. This dude was just making stuff up as we went, because I'm fairly certain I'd never been in toad pose before.

As the movements continued, the heat started to get to me. The walls seemed to be breathing, and funny lights started appearing when

I turned my head too quickly. A wave of nausea overcame me. I realized if I didn't take a break from the heat, I was gonna hurl. I left the room and went into the vestibule. The blast of refreshing cool air washed over me. The mirror across from me confirmed that I looked as if I'd just stepped out of a pool. We were only twenty minutes in. How was I going to make it through 40 more minutes of class? I sat on the bench, contemplating how ill I felt versus how much my pride demanded finishing this class. After a few minutes of marinating in my sweat, I decided I had recovered enough to head back in. I lasted exactly five more minutes before I chucked my pride out the window and gave up.

I'd never quit an exercise class in my life. I felt defeated. Maybe I was getting too old for working-out. Maybe I was just weak. Maybe I was too out of shape.

A year went by. That failure haunted me. I'm not a quitter. There was only one way to deal with this. I had to go back. I had to do hot yoga again. And this time, I would finish. The local Lifetime Fitness, where I had a membership, offered some classes. I perused through the options. As I scrolled on my phone, a small inner voice piped up with mild concern. *These class titles sound scary! With titles like "Fire," "Burn," and "Scorch," I wonder if I'll need medical attention.* Every class description sounded more daunting: activate your core with quick flow movements and a cardio blast! A cardio blast? *What is happening here?* Finally, after much scrolling, researching, and reading I found one that might be what I was looking for. The description said it was a series of deep stretches in a 100-degree room. Well, that's better than 109, I thought.

I should have known it was gonna be bad when I showed up. The line to get into the class was down the hall ending past the man with biceps the size of most people's thighs, who was on his 50th rep lifting 890 pounds.

The instructor was late and seemed surprised that all of Salt Lake City showed up for the one yoga class offered that day. Because it was hot yoga, we couldn't move to a new location. Instead, we packed in like sardines, to the point where I was sure the typical movements of raising your arms and extending your legs would look more like a game of Twister than smooth yoga moves. I took my place against the wall between two cabinets. I thought I'm small; I can fit. I did not fit.

Soon the instructor dimmed the lights, and we began what I thought would be a low, deep set of mindful stretches and some core work, but turned out to be more like a collective reproduction of a methamphetamine-induced seizure.

At that pace, I wasn't able to center myself and enjoy the pose. As I let go of my expectations of a low and slow burn and embraced the fact that I was going to have to deal with this faster pace, the instructor announced that we would now be picking up the pace EVEN MORE. We were expected to enter the pose and, at its height, immediately transition into another pose. I was actually getting winded. THIS IS YOGA!! YOU ARE NOT SUPPOSED TO BE WINDED!! This is false advertising. They said yoga, but this was aerobics!

The women in that class were over the top too. One woman did all of the poses, but upside down while balancing on a block. Another added in handstands every time our legs rose into the air. All over the room, people seemed to be magically hovering over their mats while they kicked, swung, and pressed through the moves at lightning speed. Except me. Unfortunately, my place in-between the cabinets included a mirror. Some of those images of myself trying to get into and out of those poses are gonna haunt me. And it was hot. Did I mention how hot it was? I'm basically doing some hybrid of yoga and P90X/Insanity. Sweat is dripping from every pore in my body. We were only halfway into the hour when I had downed the last of my 20 oz. water bottle.

At one point, the instructor seemed at a loss and was like, "Do whatever feels good and what your body needs." So I lay down on the floor.

I decided I had milked that long enough, and when she prompted us for the next combination, I rose to meet the challenge. Nothing was going to keep me from completing this class. (Why did I keep daring the universe like this?)

My legs began to shake as sweat dripped down my back, trailed off my forehead, and gathered in repeated drips off my nose. The room began to tilt in odd ways, and I was finding it harder and harder to balance and stay in the sequence of poses. Just when I thought it couldn't get worse, the instructor doubled down and told us to grab hands with the person next to us. That's right, grab the sweaty, dirty hand of the stranger next to you and now complete the moves with no help from your upper body. Mercifully the lights were so dim none of us could make out the other person, so at least I'll never have to know who I had to exchange bodily fluid with.

The whole yoga experience in Salt Lake City was traumatic and, quite frankly, pissed me off, but I did it. I finished the class! And I'm going to tell you right now; it was me that farted. Namaste.

# The Birds and the Bees

## *Alice M Batzel*

It only takes a few female friends getting together for lunch on a Spring afternoon to engage in conversation about all things related to the change of the season. Spring discussions often involve chatter about cute baby bunnies, chicks, ducks, lambs, blooming flowers, and butterflies. And somehow, it often expands to include more serious topics, though still seasonal to Spring. Yep. That would be the need to have "the talk" with one or more of our children. You know, the talk about "the birds and the bees," ahem, "the facts of life." That was my experience on one Spring afternoon when I met a few of my female friends for lunch at the Idle Isle Café in Brigham City, Utah.

The historic 1921 cafe was the perfect setting for sharing time-honored and modern-tested tips and techniques helpful to parents when conducting this most important discussion. Throughout generations of time, parents and kids look back on "the talk" as a rite of passage. However, both often wish it could be avoided, and it's frequently anticipated with dread. Some sail through it smoothly, and others get dry-docked somewhere along the way, usually due to loss of words, dry mouth, stammering, or delivery of misinformation on the parents' part. The ladies' Spring luncheon was going to bravely tackle the subject. Hopes were high that valuable skills would be shared by some and acquired by others. And we would be enjoying the company of one another as we savored a delicious lunch in a nostalgic family dining atmosphere. A person might think such a conversation would warrant whispers behind a closed door. Not so. The Idle Isle Café comfortably accommodated our gathering as we retreated to a back dining room. There we could engage in our discussion while we ate.

The conversation soon turned to "how we learned about the facts of life when we were kids." You can imagine the various humorous things that were shared, but there was seriousness mixed into the topic as well. I admit I did get an odd reaction from the ladies when I made a firm declaration.

"I would have to agree with Albert Einstein's statement. *The only thing that you absolutely have to know is the location of the library.*"

From the silence and blank stares, I could tell that such a declaration required explanation. I explained that when my sister and I were "of age" to receive "the talk" from our Mother, she sent us to the library and told us to go to the main desk and ask for the librarian. Mother further instructed us on what to say and what to do. I was in the sixth grade, and my sister was in the fifth. I was 13 months older than my sister, so I was designated to be the spokesperson. I was also responsible for making sure that we accomplished the task as directed by our Mother. Little did we realize, our world of knowledge was about to be dramatically changed forever.

"Our Mother sent us to the library today. Are you the librarian?" I asked.

"Yes."

"Our mother thinks that you have more knowledge than her on the mysteries of life, and she would like for you to show us some books on the subject so that my sister and I can read and learn about it," I said.

The librarian stared at us for a moment, and then she went into action. I'm not sure if she had encountered this situation before, but it was evident that our Mother was right because the librarian precisely knew what to do.

"Come with me," the librarian said. She escorted us to an aisle and pointed to a row of books.

"We can't read all of those today," I said. "We can't stay that long. What would be best for each of us?"

The librarian selected a couple of books and handed them to us.

"We might have some questions. Our Mother said that if we had any questions, we were supposed to ask the librarian because you are the expert of knowledge," I said.

The librarian stared at us again for a moment.

"I'll try to answer your questions, but if I don't have the answers, you'll have to ask your Mother."

"OK," I said, "but our Mother is pretty sure you know everything, and you have all the answers."

The librarian stared at us again, looking somewhat stunned.

"Come with me," the librarian said as she led us to a table positioned next to her desk.

"Sit here. You can read your books here."

My sister and I quietly read the books, which contained an explanation of the anatomy and physiology of human reproduction and some illustrated drawings. We could have never guessed such things. When we finished reading our books, WE HAD NO QUESTIONS for the librarian. We just wanted to go home as soon as possible.

"We're finished reading. We have to go home now," I said.

"You can just leave the books right there," said the librarian.

"Thank you. Goodbye," we said as we left the books on the desk and abruptly left the library.

As my sister and I walked home, we didn't even talk to each other. We were stunned by that trip to the library. When we arrived home, I reported to our Mother that the librarian gave us some books to read, and we read them. WE HAD NO QUESTIONS for our Mother. We didn't dare. I don't think we blinked for days.

Now that I'm a Grandmother, as I recall that experience, it brings a smile and a laugh to me. But there is a moral to this story. GOD BLESS LIBRARIANS and GOD BLESS MOTHERS WHO KNOW WHERE TO GET ANSWERS. Despite that, it's a fact, a few eyebrows raised and a few jaws dropped when I contributed to that part of the conversation during our ladies' luncheon. No one would dare doubt. Mother was a trailblazer.

Eventually, the conversation turned back to where it had first begun. The ladies wanted to share tips about how we had successfully conducted "the talk" with our children. Many positive personal experiences and much helpful information flowed back and forth between the ladies. I was amazed to witness that. My experience with the subject, however, was not so successful. I thought that if shared, perhaps it might still be helpful. I didn't have daughters. I had two sons, and I was determined not to send them to the library as I had been. Though I certainly got a thorough education with my Mother's approach, I was sure it could be improved. I enlisted the assistance of my husband. After all, it seemed proper and fitting that a Father should have those discussions with sons.

My husband was a teacher, and he was willing to discuss it with our boys when they were home from school during the summer. One of my friends had five children, and she loaned me an illustrated children's book. She and her husband felt that the book was particularly helpful when they had "the talk" with their children. The book's title was, *You Were Smaller Than A Dot*. I thought this was a genius approach to the subject. My husband was agreeable to read the book with the boys while I was at work, he would discuss it with them, and he would answer their questions. It would all be taken care of by the time I got home from work. Perfect. I thought.

When I got home from work, I was eager to find out how our plan unfolded.

"How did it go with the boys today?" I asked. "Were you all able to read the book and discuss it?"

My husband gave me no reply. He called out the oldest son's name and told him to come to the dining room where we were.

"Did you read that book that your Mother wanted you to read?" asked my husband. "Yes," our third-grade son replied.

"Do you have any questions?" my husband asked.

"No," replied our son, somewhat embarrassed.

"Do you want to talk about it?" I asked.

"No," he said rather definitely, and then returned to his bedroom to resume playing.

My husband smiled and nodded at me as though I now needed to congratulate him on being a stellar Father. I asked him if he read the book with the boys and talked to them about it. He didn't respond. He then called out the name of our younger son and asked him to come to the dining room. The second-grade son joined us, and my husband then questioned him.

"Did you read that book that your Mother wanted you to read?"

"No."

"Well, it's on the couch in the living room. Your Mother wants you to read it. Go in there and read it."

Our second-grader obediently went to the living room, plopped down on the couch, and began reading the book. I attempted to have an intelligent, though strained conversation at that point with my husband.

"I thought we planned that you were going to read the book with the boys, discuss it with them, and answer any questions that they might have," I said. "It doesn't appear like that's what happened here today. Have YOU read the book?"

"Yes. I've read the book. You're making a big deal of this, and you don't need to. Don't worry; I'm taking care of it."

In mere moments our second-grader came back to the dining room and was on his way back to his bedroom to resume playing with his brother. My husband took the opportunity to demonstrate to me that he had taken care of the education.

"Did you read the book that your Mother wanted you to read?" my husband asked.

"Yes."

"Do you have any questions?"

"No. I thought it was funny."

I was beyond exasperated by that point, and my husband knew it. He pursued further questioning.

"Why do you think it was funny?"

That is when our second-grade son began naming every person in our very fertile church congregation who was expecting a baby.

"Now I know what they've been doing. I think it's pretty funny!" our little son said as he laughed and ran down the hallway to his bedroom to resume playing.

I was about to blow my stack at that point. All I had asked was that my husband read a simple book to our sons, discuss it with them, and answer any questions that they might have. The illustrated book

19

was supposed to facilitate their discussion. It was an opportunity for a father to educate his sons before kids at school gave them a bunch of incorrect information. Now, it looked as if our younger son was going to confront every pregnant couple the next Sunday, laugh at them, and declare that he knew what they had been doing. I was horrified at the prospect and began thinking of an alternate church we could attend.

"Are you happy with how that went?" I asked my husband.

"Yes. Both boys have read the book. They don't have any questions," he replied.

I could hardly believe what I was hearing from my husband, the master's degree educator. I knew I had to take control of the situation. I called my younger son to come back to where we were.

"You're making a big deal out of nothing," my husband said under his breath.

"Fine! When our son laughs at expectant couples at church and makes fun of them, you can handle that. When he elaborates on their marital activities, you can explain to them why he thinks the idea of having families is hilarious. Especially the process required to have a family," I replied.

But somehow, I knew it would probably default to me just like it had at that very moment. I would be blind-sided in the foyer of the church with my little boy confronting a pregnant woman and her husband. He would declare that he knew all about how she got in the condition that she was. Good grief!

When our second-grader came back to the dining room, I knew I had to get this derailed experience securely back on the tracks. My husband silently observed what was transpiring.

"Daddy and I love you very much. You know that, don't you?" I said as I put my arms around my little boy.

"Yes."

"What you read in the book about having babies is not funny. It is serious. It is a very special plan from Heavenly Father so that we can have families. We should not laugh at or make fun of people when they are going to have a baby. It would hurt their feelings if you did that. Do you understand?"

"Yes."

"Promise me that you won't do that. OK?" I asked.

"OK. I promise," said my son, breaking free from my arms and running back to his bedroom to continue playing with his brother.

"You didn't need to make a big deal out of it," my husband said.

"Our mutual agreed-upon plan went off the cliff under your watch today. I have no regrets about what I did tonight. It's done. We don't need to discuss it any further," I said.

I took the book and put it with my purse so that I could return it to my friend at work the following day. I prayed for the best outcome under the circumstances. How grateful I was over the coming Sundays; my little son never confronted any expectant mothers. Thank heavens!

Many years have passed since then. Our two sons are in their 40's with children of their own. I have no idea how they conducted "the talk" with their children. But at least I'm relieved that the "birds and the bees" education that our sons received in our home did not ruin them from wanting to get married and have children when they became adults. Could our experience have been any worse? I don't know. But I find it a miracle that the human race continues to perpetuate despite how the "facts of life" education can go off-the-tracks even when intentions are good.

With all of the laughter coming from the back dining room of the Idle Isle Café that Spring afternoon, one might think that a comedy convention was underway. It was one of our more memorable ladies' luncheons for sure. What was very real that day was the realization that life happens. It's rarely the same for everyone. Somehow the experiences of life, as varied as they are, when shared, seem to bond us together. It's especially so when we share experiences as we eat a meal together. That's what happened that day. We shared our experiences about "the birds and the bees" in the comfort of that Utah diner. And through that experience, we became even more of a family with one another. Yes, I'm still laughing. But I'm even more surprised that I continue to be invited to the ladies' luncheons.

# The Poetry of Spur Nutcheck

*Jon Baty*

**The Poetry of Spur Nutcheck**

Forward by Jon Baty

Spur Nutcheck was the Bob Dylan of cowboy poetry. The brazenness of his poetry only offers you a minuscule insight into the life and mind of Spur. Born in a small country town in the early 1920s, Spur was a celebrated poet by his teens. At the age of 14, Spur had his first published poem, "Supper Time," which was lauded by critics and the elite writers of the era. Due to the poem's highly controversial themes and language, any current renditions (published or spoken) are banned in most parts of the country and a small church in Prague.

Despite his ongoing recognition, Spur spent the majority of his life on the Western prairie, herding cattle. Various celebrities, writers, and poets would travel many miles through rain, snow, and cow manure, just to bask in his presence.

In the early 1960s, Spur disappeared for the next 20 years. He called this time, "Living My Damn Life."

After his return to the scene in 1987, Spur briefly lived in La Cruz de Huanacaxtle, a small fishing village located in the state of Nayarit, north of Puerto Vallarta. During the 3 years he lived there (the "Hemingway years"), Spur was arrested 76 times but managed to write an immense volume of poetry and short stories.

Spur spent the remainder of his life at his estate outside of Bozeman, Montana. Communicating only by Northern Goshawk, he sent his poems to his agent on the first Wednesday of each month. Most of these poems were rubbish—complete rubbish. Fans often attributed the downhill of these works to his "Netflix and Chill" addictions.

In December 2019, Spur Nutcheck passed away loudly and with resistance in his sleep, but his genius and insight live on in his work.

While most of Spur's works are widely available, published, and translated, the Spur Nutcheck estate was kind enough to allow us to include these never before seen (or so his brother, Dweezil, tells us) poems.

## The Lonely Cowboy

*Life can be quite lonely,*
*When you're out there on the range.*
*Weeks and months without companionship,*
*Can make a man feel strange.*
*Your mind, it's starts to wander*
*Your feelings start to change.*
*Life can be so lonely,*
*When you're out there on the range.*

*Life can be so lonely,*
*When you're sleeping in the brush.*
*A cactus starts a'winking,*
*Which can make a cowboy blush.*
*She puts her arms up in the air,*
*Her bosom looks so plush.*
*Life can be so lonely,*
*When you're sleeping in the brush.*

*Life can be so lonely,*
*When your heart is not content.*
*The cactus can't stop flirting,*
*And you smell her lovely scent.*

*She moves her hips so lightly,*
*She is one sweet succulent.*
*Life can be so lonely,*
*When your heart is not content.*

*Life can be so lonely*
*When you're out there, I admit.*
*That cactus starts to call your name,*
*And you plead with her to quit.*
*Yet there she is before you,*
*Her body is legit.*
*Life can be so lonely,*
*When you're out there, I admit.*

*Life can be so lonely,*
*When no woman you have got.*
*16 years out in the desert,*
*Seems like an awful lot.*
*Of not knowing a woman's touch,*
*This may be your only shot*
*To make love to that cactus,*
*And holy [REDACTED], it hurts like a mother [REDACTED].*

## An Ode to My Friend, Horse

*We've shared an adventure: me and you*
*Over cattle fields and dust.*
*I know when I'm up high in my saddle*
*It's always you that I can trust.*
*I remember the time we fought that man*
*Who had shot at us and run.*
*That glint in your eye seemed to say, "go get 'em!"*
*So, we chased him to the sun.*
*Or that other time when I "accidentally" ran over that door to door salesman*
*Well, what was I to do?*
*With that glint in your eye and your horse teeth smile*

# Utah's Special Blend

*You had the same thought too.*
*We buried him in the neighbor's back yard*
*While they were gone away.*
*And when the police squad arrested them*
*"They seemed so nice," was what we'd say.*
*Or do you 'member that time we were a sniffin'*
*That powder, milky white?*
*We chased the dragon, both of us*
*That starry summer night.*
*We've had ourselves adventures*
*Been East, West, North, and South*
*But now I have to kill you*
*Cause you can't shut your tattlin' mouth.*
*"The feds, they were a pressurin' me,"*
*Is what you had to say.*
*"I swear, I cross my horse heart*
*With my horse hooves this way."*
*But my friend, we've gone too far*
*And parting is so sweet.*
*And just in case that ain't messed up enough,*
*Tonight, I dine on horse friend meat.*

## My Fourth and Only Wife

*I met her at a country fair*
*She was 6 foot 4 and change*
*My friends all said, "she's known to murder people!"*
*But love don't see deranged*

*I took her on the ferris wheel*
*She didn't seem too scary*
*Even though her dress was covered in stuff*
*Like from that movie "Carrie"*

*I married her that fall*

# Jon Baty

*"In the woods," her only wish*
*My best man was my gambling buddy*
*Her maid of honor: rotting fish*

*As we held hands, the preacher asked*
*Do you take each other, no fault?*
*I looked at you and said, "I do"*
*and you said, "I smell salt."*

*And then you tried to murder us*
*But I couldn't help but see*
*That look of romance in your eye*
*When you were chasing me*

*My gambling buddy shot at you*
*And you yelled at him to run*
*Your voice had dropped into a growl*
*Which made it much more fun*
*Then the preacher came behind you*
*And got you into a choke hold*
*He's never seen such awfulness*
*To the FBI is what he told*

*I'm almost certain you were possessed*
*But my love for you is true*
*And if you ever get out of San Quentin*
*I'll be waiting here for you*

## Increments of Time

*Time is merely an illusion,*
*Is what's been often said.*
*And increments of time measured,*
*Is what's been going through my head.*

*20 minutes is what I've found*
*To tie a lasso that won't break.*
*23 more minutes it can last*
*When your rope is a live rattlesnake.*

*Drinking Old Milwaukee with my dog,*
*Rico is abrasive.*
*Over time, it takes three beers in him,*
*Before he gets too racist.*

*The scariest time in my whole life,*
*I concede was not that smart.*
*I only spent 4 minutes*
*Past 10 pm in a WalMart.*

*It's never wasting one's time,*
*Watching clouds above, so high.*
*The most important time I've taken*
*Is binge watching NCIS and CSI.*

*I wrote this poem in 7 minutes,*
*Not the greatest, I'll admit.*
*But it was written, whilst I was sittin'*
*On the throne, taking a [REDACTED].*

# Social Distancing, Psychology, and Straitjackets

## *James D Beers*

Apparently, *The Young and the Restless* is older than I am. And I only know this because, by late-March, the situation had turned so far south that I found myself sitting on the couch in my wife's bathrobe watching the fabled soap on the iPad and googling its history on a smartphone.

At two in the afternoon.

Usually, I'm out of my wife's bathrobe by at least seven in the morning.

But that's not even the worst of it. We hadn't left our apartment in Ogden or ventured off the path to our backyard storage shed save one trip to the grocery store in three weeks. The household's digestive tracts were plugged up with food storage vittles (I swore if my wife Jenna made another batch of homemade bread, I'd poop loaves and fart flour), hygiene somehow went out with the garbage ("This place smells weird!"), and the couch cushions were developing permanent butt divots ("Scoot over, mine doesn't fit here."). All in all, it felt like a leper colony and reeked of Boy Scout camp and ripe hamper.

Personally, I hadn't even made it two days into the COVID-19's social distancing mandate before I cracked. Sure, I had plenty to do— I had the office laptop for teleworking, YouTube videos, and Vudu movies were at my fingertips, more books than I could read in a year lined our bookshelves, and we had games out the wazoo.

But none of it was helpful.

Perhaps heinie fatigue from sitting on my duff all day long eventually overtook me. Maybe one-too-many Monopoly sessions finally frayed the last wire connected to my sanity. It could've also been our one-and-only teenager's perpetual statement of boredom. Seriously, every five minutes—"I'm bored!" It was like the persistent and eternal drip-drop of Chinese water torture. Owing to my compromised state, I once told him to go out in the street and find some COVID zombies to fight.

Whatever the cause of my near lunacy, I was two marbles shy of drooling all over myself and babbling incoherently.

So I turned to NAMI Utah, the state's chapter, division, or whatever-the-fetch-you-want-to-call-it of the National Alliance on Mental Illness (hence NAMI)*. I figured their website would help me self-diagnose and maybe even had some recipes for do-it-yourself anti-anxiety concoctions. You know, like two parts milkweed, half a banana, twelve parts vodka (hey, if it's medicinal, it's okay for us Latter-day Saints…right?).

Anyway, one thing led to another, and I determined I had apotemnophilia, or an overwhelming desire to amputate healthy parts of my body.

No, not really. But it certainly was an education on mental disorders that plague the human race**.

Near as I could tell, from my long walk through the web, I was definitely experiencing some anxiety and probably a bit of depression.

Dagnabbit! As if the coronavirus wasn't enough!

So I watched *What About Bob?* that comedy flick with Bill Murray and Richard Dreyfuss that's kind of about mental illness. I figured it would be good therapy and thought perhaps Dreyfuss's psychologist's character might even say something that could calm the frazzle and lift me out of the dumps.

Funny stuff! I laughed a lot, and it made me feel better.

Until I returned to teleworking and the endless wrestle with long-distance technology.

Not even Bill Murray can cheer up my company's Eeyore-ish VPN (i.e., virtual private network, or in this case, virtual piece o' number two). Seriously, it's more sluggish than a slug. I've seen glaciers move faster than this thing. We could reinstate the Pony

Express and send information faster by horse. It was both nerve-wracking and depressing.

"You stupid piece of—" I wanted to swear at it. In fact, I probably did...multiple times. But in my distressed state, I don't remember any of it. I could just as well have been praying for a miracle—I didn't know the difference.

"James, maybe you should take a fifteen-minute break," Jenna suggested during one of my computer tirades. "You've been sitting at the computer for hours."

"AARRROOOWEEOOW!" I growled. Incoherency had set in. The situation was reaching dire levels.

Despite not wanting to, I took my wife's advice. I got on the Internet from my home computer—just for a few minutes!—to find and print out a couple of psychological screening tests I'd seen in my previous mental health search. I was determined to figure out what the heck was wrong with me, and taking these tests, I knew, would give me an answer.

But I got sidetracked on mantherapy.org***.

Now, this I could get into, I thought. Here was a Nick Offerman lookalike giving practical yet humorous mental health advice to stressed-out, depressed, manly men like myself (yes, that's right, I kiss my biceps...what man doesn't?).

"...you'll have tools you need to deal with the tough situations life sends your way," he says, "like breakups, layoffs, and your pain-in-the-ass teenager." Okay, so he missed pandemic isolation, but he got the other one in there.

This guy—this Dr. Rich Mahogany (or whoever was behind his creation)—was a genius! Who would have thought humor could be an answer to mental health challenges? Perhaps that was it; maybe funny stuff was my therapy.

"HUMOR!" I screamed and then laughed maniacally.

Mantherapy.org had inspired me! With a pen and some freshly-printed psychological screening tests, I left my computer desk, went downstairs, and plopped down at the kitchen table to begin answering questions.

***

*Tell us a bit about yourself:*
*- What age are you?*
Prehistoric. Devonian, to be exact—the age of fishes!
(I chuckled despite myself.)

*- Which gender do you identify most with?*
Male…no, female!…no, male! Yes, male…but that kind of confuses my answer to the next question.
(Oh, boy!)

*- Are you pregnant or planning to become pregnant in the next three to six months?*
Yes, I think so…That's definitely why that big "something" is hanging over my belt. It's not ice cream! I repeat—it's <u>NOT</u> ice cream!
(Ha, ha, HAAA!)

*In the past four weeks…*
*…about how often did you feel tired-out for no good reason?*
*(circle one only)*
  *1. None of the time*
  *2. A little of the time*
  *3. Some of the time*
  *4. Most of the time*
  *5. All of the time*
I circled number one only, but it doesn't apply. I see fluffy bunnies.
(Ooh, that's good—hee, hee, hee!)

*In the past four weeks…*
*…about how often did you feel nervous? (circle one only)*
  *1. None of the time*
  *2. A little of the time*
  *3. Some of the time*

*4. Most of the time*
*5. All of the time*

I'm a man, and I shake so badly I have to sit down when I go pee. (HA! HAAA!)

### *In the past four weeks...*
### *...about how often did you feel hopeless? (circle one only)*

*1. None of the time*
*2. A little of the time*
*3. Some of the time*
*4. Most of the time*
*5. All of the time*

Help me, Obi-Wan Kenobi, you're my <u>ONLY</u> hope! P.S.—Where are my droids?

(Hee, hee!)

### *In the past four weeks...*
### *...about how often did you feel that everything was an effort? (circle one only)*

*1. None of the time*
*2. A little of the time*
*3. Some of the time*
*4. Most of the time*
*5. All of the time*

Everything...except eating ice cream... P.S.—This form is an effort...

(Take that—ha, ha!)

### *In the past four weeks...*
### *...about how often have you had trouble falling or staying asleep? (circle one only)*

*1. None of the time*
*2. A little of the time*
*3. Some of the time*
*4. Most of the time*
*5. All of the time*

All the flippin' time! My wife is a doggone werewolf!
(HAA, HA, HA, HAAAA!!!)

### *In the past four weeks...*
*...about how often have you felt a loss of interest in activities that you used to enjoy?* (circle one only)
1. None of the time
2. A little of the time
3. Some of the time
4. Most of the time
5. All of the time

I no longer enjoy ice cream—PLEASE HELP MEEEEEEE!!!
(HEE, HEE! Oh man, that would be terrible!)

### *In the past four weeks...*
*...about how often have you not been able to stop or control worrying?* (circle one only)
1. None of the time
2. A little of the time
3. Some of the time
4. Most of the time
5. All of the time

The lady at the desk said this form would only take a few minutes. I'm going on five! What do I do? What do I do? What do I do? What do I do?
(BWAA, HAAA!!!)

### *In the past four weeks...*
*...about how often have you felt distant or cut off from other people?* (circle one only)
1. None of the time
2. A little of the time
3. Some of the time
4. Most of the time
5. All of the time

Uh…my parents live on a beach in Greece…I live in Arkansas…Thanks, thanks a lot for reminding me.

(Ooh—ha, ha, ha!)

### In the past four weeks...

*…about how often have you had trouble concentrating on things such as reading the newspaper or watching television?* *(circle one only)*

1. *None of the time*
2. *A little of the time*
3. *Some of the time*
4. *Most of the time*
5. *All of the time*

What was that? I forgot the question…something about…Hey, this pen is from the bank—did you guys steal this? Speaking of banks—I wonder if they still give out suckers?

(HA!…wait…there's probably some truth to this one…)

### In the past four weeks...

*…about how often have you had diarrhea, constipation, or other digestive problems?* *(circle one only)*

1. *None of the time*
2. *A little of the time*
3. *Some of the time*
4. *Most of the time*
5. *All of the time*

Yes…I hope you brought some Glade or Febreeze or something.

(BWAAAA! Nothing like a good digestive joke!)

### In the past four weeks...

*…about how often have you had a poor appetite or found yourself overeating?* *(circle one only)*

1. *None of the time*
2. *A little of the time*
3. *Some of the time*
4. *Most of the time*

*5. All of the time*

I only overeat on Thursdays, 'cause that's when the tapeworms are active.

(*Snort, snort*—I love doing this!)

\*\*\*

Holy mackerel! What a FANTASTIC first therapy session! Writing out hilarious answers to psychological screening test questions—and, of course, laughing about it!—was THE BEST! In fact, it worked so well that I printed out a stack of blank tests and kept them on the kitchen table for when I needed a little boost. I didn't throw away any of the completed tests either; turns out reading the old answers was almost as cathartic as writing new ones.

Eventually, I got the whole family into it. Whenever each of us took a break, we'd fill out a question sheet and leave it on the kitchen table to read during dinner. We'd laugh so hard that mac n' cheese, meatloaf, spaghetti, General Tso's Spicy Chicken, whatever we were eating sprayed out our mouths and came out our noses with every guffaw.

Not only was our new-found therapy great for quelling depression and anxiety with each test, but our collective creativity also soared, generating even funnier answers. On several sheets, I complained about winged-cow hallucinations and a strange case of compulsive swearing whenever I worked on cars or wore argyle socks. Our son Joseph worked up some answers about a nervous stomach-churning out diarrhea so atrocious he called it the "butt dry heaves." Jenna's answers, though, topped them all. On one test, she insisted she had disco fever so intense that her left ear persistently heard ABBA, her right ear couldn't get rid of the Bee Gees, and every night she YMCA-ed her keister right out of bed.

\*\*\*

Answering psychological screening tests had gone on for about a week, just into early April, when I noticed a half dozen of my

35

completed sheets were missing. I intended to put the whole lot of them in a scrapbook about our experience during the COVID-19 pandemic (it's for posterity—they'll love it!).

"Hey! Have either of you guys seen the set of tests with the 'I can't feel my face' and 'fear of lint' answers?" I asked Jenna and Joseph. "I can't seem to find them."

"No, haven't seen 'em for a few days," Joseph answered.

"I haven't seen them either," Jenna said. "Did you look in the kitchen counter box?"

Of course, Jenna kept all the important stuff in a plastic box on the kitchen counter. I looked, but they weren't there either. No matter, I thought, I remembered what I'd written and could redo them. I didn't give them another thought.

Until the following Monday, April 6.

By then, I'd been working from home since March 16 and, along with answering a couple dozen psychological test questions, had created a spreadsheet to calculate the cost savings of toilet paper rationing.

Joe's school had started remote learning around the same time I started teleworking (at least I think so—honestly, I wasn't paying attention). In his spare time (i.e., when he wasn't *attempting* to work on school), he turned into an origami-folding freakazoid (don't come to visit us…we're paper crane hoarders!).

Jenna dusted off some old recipe books—*101 Dried Bean Bakes*, *Crock-Pot in Times of Chaos*, and *Soylent Green: Last Ingredients for the Last Days*. I subsequently tried to hide them (we only had so much toilet paper). She had also started laying out a commemorative quilt made entirely of homemade COVID-19 face masks (maybe she needs a mental health check—is there a womantherapy.org?).

Let's just say life was moving along slowly—v-e-r-y s-l-o-w-l-y— as in the hours were dawdling by and we were…let's face it, bored out of our flippin' gourds! Like watch-paint-dry bored!

And just when things couldn't get any more "exciting," that's when, as they say in the scriptures, all hell broke loose ("And behold, all hell broke loose" —I think it's in the New Testament…or maybe the Old Testament?).

Halfway through my 953rd trip to the refrigerator (for the day, that is—953rd trip for the day), I heard the siren.

It sounded close, I thought. Maybe on our street. I turned toward the living room window to see Joe and Jenna already there peeking through the Venetian blinds.

"It's an ambulance," Joe declared.

"Uh oh," Jenna gasped. "They're stopping in front of the Dankworths."

"Really?" I rushed to the window to see for myself. The Dankworths were a retired couple across the street who went to church with us and, during less-calamitous times (and less-contagious, I might add), obsessed over their hedges.

Reaching over Jenna and Joe, I spread a crack between some blind slats just in time to see a couple of super-thick Islanders step out of the ambulance cab.

"Those dudes are HUGE," Joe remarked.

"Yeah, good thing they brought reinforcements." I loved sarcasm. "I don't know how they'll lift the Dankworths into the back of that ambulance. I mean, Old Danks and his wife gotta weigh like a buck fifty combined." I chuckled a couple...chucks?...and then noticed Grizzly Bear and his brother Yeti coming toward our place. I left the window to spy through the front door peephole.

"Wait," Joe said, still at the window. "There's another big guy getting outta the back. Looks like he's carrying a big jacket...with...um...straps, maybe?"

"James...?" I barely caught the apprehension in Jenna's voice before the doorbell rang, and I opened the door.

"Good afternoon—"

"The Dankworths live over there," I interrupted Grizzly Bear, pointing between him and Yeti at the house across the street.

"We're not here to see the Dankworths," Griz continued. "Are you Mr. James Beers?"

"Yes," I said, intentionally suspicious.

"The same James Beers who suffers from," he briefly looked down at his clipboard, "facial numbness, trichophobia, compulsive swearing tics, winged-cow hallucinations, butt dry heaves—"

Griz stopped abruptly and tried to look over my shoulder just as I heard a soft thud behind me.

Jenna had fainted. And Joe? He must've skedaddled, for he was no longer in the living room.

Before I could rush to Jenna's side, Griz grabbed me by the shoulder.

"Benny, take care of her. We'll load this one."

Benny—aka Yeti—squeezed past me and began trying to wake Jenna.

"Wait…did you say load this—" Griz pulled me out the door and into the arms of Kong, the third Polynesian paramedic.

"Don't worry, Mr. Beers. She'll call you at the hospital."

My protests might have been more convincing had that darn compulsive swearing tic not been so prevalent.

The next thing I knew, I was strapped to a gurney in an ambulance and looking pleadingly out the back door at my now-revived wife.

"I'll call you, okay, Honey?" Jenna waved from the street.

"Wait, wait—" I was gonna ask her to tell Griz, Benny, and Kong that the facial numbness, the winged-cow hallucinations, the butt dry heaves were all a big misunderstanding, but Benny closed the door.

Suddenly I had what I can only describe as a bout of acute Coprolalia (i.e., sailor's Tourette's, if you catch my drift).

***

Four days later, I had calmed down enough to chuckle at my predicament. Apparently, Joe had mailed several of my completed psychological tests to the hospital as an April Fools' joke, expecting the hospital to call back, and we could all have a good laugh over the funny answers.

At the time, I did not see the humor in it. Jenna suggested I take a few days to cool off before I talked to Joe, and maybe I could laugh by then. The psychiatrist also thought that was a good idea, just like she thought going over several of my bogus tests each day was a good idea.

"We just want to be on the safe side," she said from the plastic chair in my psych wardroom, "and make sure none of these conditions are present before you go home."

I think we're down to the last couple tests, but if I'm not mistaken, they're doozies—a severe case of lycanthropy (as indicated by two hairy patches on my back and enough arm hair to weave a rug) and my left eye sees everything as black-and-white silent movies. In contrast, my right eye sees people as Eskimos.

Not sure if I'll pass this one. I had a hard enough time convincing the psychiatrist that the fluffy bunnies were brown, not white.

---

*Author's Note: Some individuals may see mental illness and humor as worlds apart like they should not even be connected. I can understand that. While I don't think mental illness is funny itself, I certainly try to laugh *in* it and have found humor an important part of my own therapy.

I've suffered with clinical major depressive disorder since 2014 and have likely had generalized anxiety disorder since my late teens. Twice I've been hospitalized for mental illness—the first time for severe depression and suicidal ideation, the second time for severe panic attacks. The first time, I admitted myself to the hospital. The second time, an ambulance and firetruck arrived to take me to the hospital as neither I nor my wife could get me into the car (my panic attacks include extreme claustrophobia). All of the doctors, hospital staff, counselors, psychologists, spiritual leaders, friends, family, and medications have been essential components of therapy that I could not do without. However, I feel the same way about humor. I certainly can't always laugh about depression or anxiety, nor do I think that's totally necessary. Nonetheless, I do try to find humor during the experience, whether outside the source in a funny book or movie or finding the ridiculous in some of my thought patterns or especially in self-deprecating humor.

Another thing I find helpful when I'm struggling with depression and anxiety is talking about it. I talk openly about my mental health challenges with my family, in church, at work, and on social media. I don't think it's any more shameful than having appendicitis or a broken leg. In 2019, I delivered a talk on depression and anxiety to my church congregation. If you're interested, you can find the talk here:

https://www.facebook.com/james.d.beers/posts/1015683958942560 9

Although I introduce NAMI Utah in a humorous way, I'm not trying to make fun of it. The National Alliance on Mental Illness Utah (NAMI Utah) is a phenomenal resource for those suffering mental illness and for those who know someone suffering from mental illness. They offer free in-person and online courses for teens and adults, online support groups, support for families, friends, and caregivers of military service members with mental illness, suicide prevention, and suicide loss resources, access to Family Resource Facilitators, literature on managing mental illness crises, and access to other entities providing mental health services. I find the *Navigating a Mental Health Crisis* guide very helpful.

The Church of Jesus Christ of Latter-day Saints also has many online resources available for anyone, regardless of whether or not they are members of the church. I especially like the videos they post relating other's experiences with mental health challenges.

**Author's Note: The gamut of human maladies, let alone mental and behavioral disorders is unbelievable. There is a lot of human suffering in the world, which can be overwhelmingly disheartening. In my own short lifetime, I've seen many people experiencing severe mental illnesses, and I truly feel and pray for them. When working with and diagnosing patients with mental illnesses, professionals in the mental health field, use the Diagnostic and Statistical Manual of Mental Disorders, which is updated every so often. The Internet can be a good place to search for information on mental health, but be sure to reference reputable sites, like those for NAMI, the National Institute for Mental Health, the Center for Disease Control and Prevention, WebMD, the Mayo Clinic, and the American Psychological Association among others.

Fact: apotemnophilia, or an overwhelming desire to amputate healthy parts of one's body, although rare, is a real mental disorder.

***Author's Note: I love mantherapy.org because it incorporates humor into understanding and managing stress and mental illness, particularly depression and anxiety. The resource is geared toward men who struggle to share anything that has to do with feelings, although I think it's useful for anyone who has a mental illness. Even if you don't have a mental illness, I recommend you check it out as it is quite entertaining while at the same time educational.

# Don't Let Trucks Get You In Trouble

## *DeAnne Mattix*

I think I've got dance somewhere in my soul; it's just that it's never had any idea how to come out through my body. I spent my adolescence strenuously avoiding all social invitations that might present even the slight possibility of having to drag my inelegant body onto a dance floor. I just didn't *get* the idea of going through a series of repetitious gyrations in the name of musical appreciation.

Though I survived the high school years unscathed, I soon discovered that choosing to attend a religious college campus in Utah meant my days were numbered. When my roommates got wind of my disinclinations, they plotted their best to set me up on a date that would include dancing in the course of the evening. By an awful stroke of luck, they finally got their chance.

Ed came along.

For the longest time, I didn't even know him as an actual person—I just knew his truck. I've always had a thing for Ford pickups sitting up high on a lift kit, sporting big old mud tires, and a roll bar with KC lights. For months I had passed this particular truck on the way to chem lab, always stopping to admire my dream vehicle up close and personal. I never knew who owned it since I never saw it driven—just parked.

When the prom was only a week away, I got caught red-handed admiring The Dream Truck. A tall (and I *do* mean tall) farm boy came sauntering up. This is what I immediately noticed: High-water pants. Tissue-paper tabs still clinging to his hit-and-miss shave job of that morning. Adam's apple the size of a Valencia orange poking over his collar. And the most awkward-looking homemade bowl cut ever. I guess I'd envisioned someone like Patrick Swayze or maybe even Tom Selleck to be driving such a truck.

"Somethin' wrong with my tires?" he asked.

"Uh…nope. Nope, they look just fine. Nice truck," I managed to stammer before I scuttled away, blushing.

How was I to know one of my roommates had seen the embarrassing interchange?

Three days later, Mr. Bowl Cut showed up at my door with enormous bouquets of both flowers *and* balloons, inviting me to go to the prom with him. I was incredulous. How had he found out where I lived? Somehow, I'd been certain every single male on campus must have heard through the grapevine by now that I was the last—the very last—person to ask to a dance.

"Of course, she'll go with you!" announced my roomie, surging past my stuttering self at the door and grabbing the overstated gifts. It was all over before I could find my voice or shut my flytrap. I was left to console myself that at least I'd get to ride in The Dream Truck.

My roommates went into an immediate tizzy of mother hen-ism. All semester they had been attempting to "turn me into a girl." As a committed tomboy, I hadn't been at all perturbed to show up for college life in worn Levis and my brother's cast-off T-shirts. I wore my hair in an uncomplicated ponytail or messy bun (this, amidst the mile-high hairdos of the eighties) and eschewed makeup.

The roomies had only recently trapped me in the apartment, cut my hair, forced me to learn the basic rudiments of curling iron technology, and plastered me with makeup. My birthday gifts from them had been an entirely new "shared" girly-girl wardrobe. I was still trying to acclimate myself to things like fuchsia and lace.

Shopping for a prom dress became the next phase of their frenzied feminization project. I ended up having to borrow a long slip and dressy shoes. They were horrified when I suggested I could get away with my casual loafers and not invest in glitzy footwear. I just couldn't manage to convince them that shoes were no big deal—why, they'd barely even show under the hem of the pale blue gown they'd chosen.

Ed—yes, driving The Dream Truck—showed up late. Even his tux britches were high water level. Apparently, his skinny legs had even eluded the ministrations of our local tailors. The toilet-paper tabs were missing, but the bowl cut had now been chopped to an alarming degree of shortness, leaving gleaming whitewalls around his sunburned face and neck. Prince Charming, he might not have been, but he was polite and attentive.

I hadn't taken into consideration the lift-kit on the truck. Climbing in would have been a cinch in Levi's, but I was stuck with yards and yards of fabric billowing in one of the strongest windstorms of the season. I could feel my carefully coiffed hair spinning into a disaster despite having been thoroughly shellacked into place with industrial-strength Aqua-Net.

I noticed Ed had been thoughtful enough to move most of the hay, ropes, and tools to the center of the front seat between us. Off we went in nervous anticipation. Little did I know my worries over my failing bouffant would soon pale in comparison to what waited just moments ahead.

As soon as we parked, Ed jumped out of his side of the truck and ran around to sweep open my door gallantly. For some reason— probably fearing the awkwardness of a moist hand helping me to the ground-- I decided to leap gracefully from the cab. I hadn't planned on the dress ballooning up in a mighty gust of wind and catching on the manual roll-up handle for the truck window. Yes, I flew through the air gracefully-- but only until the fabric of both gown and borrowed slip met the limits of their endurance, and a horrifying *r-i-i-p* sounded as both tore from ground level to my hip.

Ed, to his credit, looked the other way while I tried—in gale-force winds—to gather the errant fabric to cover my now-exposed lower body. I felt a sudden deep appreciation for the glitzy dress shoes. Somehow, we made it inside, and I fled to the ladies' room to survey the damage.

No way could I dance like this.

Other girls, looking composed and elegant with their perfectly retouched hair and intact ball gowns, passed me without a look. No one offered to help. I had just decided I might be spending the rest of my natural-born days sitting in that chair in the ladies' room when an angel of mercy appeared. Of all people, it was the college president's wife who showed up, and—wonder of wonders—she had an entire package of safety pins in her purse. What were the chances of that??

Together we pulled and pinned, tucked, and gathered. At last, we found an arrangement of folds that mostly hid the damage. My new-found mentor assured me I'd be able to carry this off if I avoided high-energy tangos or foxtrots—no worries in that department.

Ed was waiting in the hall, looking anxious.

The dance had already started. We stopped at the photo booth and had our portrait taken (while I skillfully hid the pinned disaster just out of view of the camera) and then entered the dance hall. As we merged in amongst the other dancers, I kept mentally reassuring myself, *"It's only three hours. It's only three hours."*

Ed, taller than me by about two flagpoles or so, folded himself over my shoulder rather like an old roll of carpet stored in the corner of a garage. He was heavy. He was sweaty. And about eight bars into the first song, he started sniffling. *Loudly.* Then, even more loudly and more frequently.

Allergies, I thought.

Then he startled me by braying into my ear, "Oh, my heck! OHMYHECK!"

The carpet unfurled itself, and I was presented with his horror-stricken face sporting the most epic nosebleed of the century. He was aghast and started wiping the sleeves of his rented tux back and forth across his face. The couples immediately surrounding us parted and stepped back in alarm as the gym floor became spotted with bright crimson blood.

"Look at her dress!" one of the princesses next to me said. Her expression of disgust was impressive, but though I looked, I could only see a couple of small spots of blood near my right shoulder. It was then I realized most people were moving around to stare at the *back* of my dress. I finally craned my neck around to check out my reflection in the mirrors along the wall. There was enough blood on the back of my dress to make it look like there was a murder in progress.

45

Ed was bobbing his head, cupping his hands under his gushing nose. "Oh, man! I'm so sorry. Someone just bag my head!"

Like Cinderella, I fled. Ed apologized about a thousand times on the drive home, even though I reassured him over and over, "No worries. No problem. It's okay." We exchanged a sticky handshake, and then The Dream Truck roared away.

Since all my roomies were still at the dance, and miraculously none of them had witnessed my total social annihilation, I threw the dress in the tub to soak. Then I climbed into my favorite Levi's and a Tee and pulled my ruined hairdo into a comfortable messy bun.

To heck with being a girly-girl, I decided. I untied one of the pink balloons Ed had brought over and slowly inhaled a good lungful of helium.

*"My one and only prom,"* I chirped to myself in the mirror. *"Been there; done that."*

# Field Lions

## *Mike Nelson*

In Northern Utah, there is a federal migratory bird refuge that, at certain times during the year, plays host to literally millions of migratory birds. In the summertime, hundreds of species of birds come here to mate and raise their young.

Every refuge, unfortunately, has its share of predators. These predators come in many forms, sizes, and tenacity. Early in the spring, when the birds are nesting, raccoons, skunks, mice, rats, snakes, crows, magpies, hawks, eagles, and even seagulls pray upon the nests, destroying many tens of thousands of eggs. Many nocturnal predators find nesting birds virtually defenseless at night and devour them in their nests, and often their young with wild abandon.

Trying to keep the predators in balance, so the refuge remains exactly that – a refuge – becomes a never-ending battle. Because using poisons is never a good alternative, refuge employees often have to resort to what you might call "mechanical removal" methods. Those methods involve trapping (both live and lethal trapping methods), and more often than not, the use of firearms (It's a little hard to trap a flying predator).

Unfortunately, predator control often becomes a serious point of controversy. Animal rights advocates champion causes such as live trapping, spay and neuter programs, etc., to control the four-footed predators. The problem is, at the end of the day, what happens to an animal who has been caught and rendered sterile? Advocates would have them returned to the refuge to continue preying on the birds.

So what, you might ask, becomes of those less affectionate critters who are caught in said live traps? Well, let me put it this way. What does one do with a forty-pound, very angry raccoon? Nobody wants that in their back yards so – well, you get the picture.

Not often recognized as true predators, the refuge is also called home by literally hundreds of feral housecats. Most of these "*pussycats*" come from – you got it – *your* homes. Hundreds of unwanted cats each year are taken for a little ride out in the country where they are set free by their well-meaning but uninformed owners to *live in the wilds*. No problem, you say. There's got to be plenty to eat out there – right? The first problem is many have never learned to hunt, and they starve. The ones who do survive evolve from the friendly little lap cat you had scampering around your living room chasing yarn balls to a stealthy, hardened, quick, and vicious ball of teeth and claws. These "born-again" tabby cats truly become *lions* in the field.

When you consider the cat's plight and what made them that way, it's truly a shame to have to remove them mechanically, but refuge managers have few other choices. It has been estimated that at any given time, there are well over four-hundred of these *lions* roaming the local refuge. If these *lions* restricted their foraging to rodents and snakes, they might help control some of the other predator problems, but eggs and baby birds are all so much easier to catch – and eat.

Enter the *lion* hunter – we'll call him Albert.

Now in his younger years, Albert raised and trained a pack of lion hounds. He and his many friends employed those hounds in the mountains where they legally treed and dispatched much larger versions of a housecat — cougars. Now that Albert was somewhat past his prime, he still loved raising hounds but had limited his kennel to a single well-trained, prime-of-his-life lion hound he called Ringo.

Albert was employed by the refuge to control the number of *field lions* roaming the refuge, but there was a stipulation attached. He couldn't ply his trade while the birds were nesting and raising their young because Ringo would disturb the nesting birds. Albert couldn't ply his trade when the waterfowl hunters were in the field either, for obvious reasons. That left Albert at the refuge in the dead of winter when most, if not all, of the sloughs and channels, were frozen over.

Times were hard for the *lions* after Christmas because there were no eggs, no defenseless young chicks, and worse yet, many adult birds had migrated to warmer climes. Besides, virtually no self-respecting rodent would present themselves above the snow where the ever-present hawks and owls could spot them. These same times, however, were the very best for Albert and Ringo for a couple of reasons. Lions can't travel without leaving tracks in the snow, and *lions* can be easily spotted on the snowy landscape anytime they're not hunkered down in the rushes.

Albert set off for the refuge on a freezing-cold but crystal-clear January morning to hunt *lions*. To be protected from the stinging cold and harsh winter winds, Albert was sporting a brand-new goose-down parka, new insulated gloves, Insulated overalls, and a fur-lined hat with earmuffs that tied down under his chin to keep the hat in place in the wind.

Ringo, of course, was the first arrow in Albert's quiver. The dog was fleet of foot and virtually fearless when facing any feline. In the event Ringo tired out or happened to be out-maneuvered by a fleeing *lion*, Albert resorted to his second arrow, his twelve-gauge Remington 870 Wingmaster, pump shotgun. From prior experience, Albert knew that one or the other would be equally effective in fulfilling his charter as *chief field lion* hunter on the refuge.

Albert drove slowly along the first dike that crisp morning, watching for telltale *lion* tracks. The stinging north wind had piled up heavy snowdrifts on the down-wind side of the dike and even drifted over a lot of the cattails alongside the road. Almost as far as Albert could see lay a sparkling sea of white. Just as they were nearing the far side of the first dike, Albert spotted a dark something, some two hundred yards or so out on the iced-over slough. At first, he thought it might be a wounded or stranded bird. But then, as he stopped and watched, he realized he was only half right. There was, in fact, a bird out on the ice, but there was also a *lion* that had been feeding on the stricken bird.

Smiling confidently to himself, Albert stepped out of his truck, loaded his shotgun, and freed Ringo.

Now Ringo had played this game before. He knew it was his job to circle, then engage the *lion,* so as it ran to evade him, it would be driven back towards Albert, who could then end its dash for freedom with the twelve gauge.

Albert stepped out on the ice at the edge of the slough, so he would have an unfettered view of the chase and be ready with his shotgun at the moment of truth, as the *lion* scrambled into the tulles in an attempt to evade Ringo.

Ringo played his part perfectly, not even approaching the lion until he had placed himself between his quarry and the far side of the slough.

The *lion* had also been playing its part well, crouching so low on the ice that if it had been white, instead of black, it might have become nearly invisible on the snow-covered ice.

Ringo was not fooled, however, and suddenly charged, baying a song long practiced by his breed when in hot pursuit.

Two hundred yards may have seemed like a considerable distance, but if a person can run a hundred yards in under ten seconds, you can imagine how little time it takes for a scrambling, highly-motivated *lion* to cover the same distance.

On they came! Albert raised his shotgun to his shoulder but then realized he had a serious problem. Instead of heading broadside for the tulles, as Albert had anticipated, the *lion* was streaking straight towards him in a blinding burst of speed. Worse yet, Ringo was baying his chase song less than ten yards behind, clearly in the path of Alberts shotgun blast.

Then Albert realized he had another, far more severe problem. Cats often look for a tree when being pursued by a lion hound, and there were no trees on the refuge – at least not within scrambling distance of the streaking *lion*. At just over six-feet tall, Albert was clearly the tallest structure around. Not knowing what to do, Albert did nothing.

Incredibly, the cat went airborne when it was still over twenty-feet away. Albert dropped his shotgun and covered his face with his arms. He didn't know whether the cat caught hold of his padded arms first or simply landed atop his head. At any rate, the lion sunk its claws into Albert's hat and held on for dear life. Ringo arrived moments later, snarling, baying, circling, and leaping into the air in an attempt to snatch the *lion* off Albert's head.

The *lion* swirled around atop Albert's head in an attempt to keep his teeth and claws facing into Ringo's attack. In so doing, the cat's claws shredded Albert's new insulated cap, sending tufts of fur torn from the inside of the cap floating down all around Albert's shoulders. In moments, the cat's claws tore through the cap and began slicing into Albert's bald head.

Ordinarily, one would have to untie the earmuffs from beneath one's chin to rip off the fur-lined hat. Albert somehow managed to snatch the cat, *and* the hat, off his battered head in one panic-stricken movement, flinging them both several feet off into the snow.

Once dislodged from his lofty perch, the *lion* realized he had but one option, and that was to climb back up the "*tree.*"

Up the front of Albert's body, the cat scrambled. Luckily, Albert was already protecting his face with his arms and elbows as the cat clawed its way up his body. Goose down flew like jetsam in a pillow fight as Albert fought to keep the lion away from his face, and the *lion* fought valiantly to reach the top of the "*tree.*"

Albert won the first heat by grabbing the lion by the head and flinging it down in the snow.

Ringo instantly gave chase, and this time the lion clawed its way up the back of Albert's insulated coveralls and then up the back of his new parka.

Albert flung his arms over his head as the *lion* topped the *tree* again and sank its claws into the padded arms of his coat.

Albert felt now as if he was fighting for his life against this thrashing, yowling, ball of fur, teeth, and claws. With a blood-curdling scream, he thrust his arms straight up over his head and swung the cat away from his body. The lion tore free, but not without taking with it several layers of quilted cloth and freeing a small snowstorm of goose down.

The lion barely touched the ground before it came for Albert again.

Having little now to protect himself from the cat, Albert ducked his head and turned his back.

Both Ringo and the cat hit him simultaneously, knocking him down face-first into the snow.

Then suddenly,+ it was over. Albert was no longer the tallest structure on the slough, and both the cat and Ringo were gone.

Still dazed by the encounter and burning from a dozen deep bites and scratches, Albert lay face down in the snow for a few long moments wondering – no praying – that it was over.

Then Albert became aware of Ringo's incessant baying. The dog had treed the *lion* somewhere. The wounded, ragged, old hunter struggled to his feet and looked around. Ringo was nowhere in sight. The foot-print riddled snow all around him was littered with puffs of hat fur, goose down, and shredded cloth. Worse yet, the snow was also dotted here and there by crimson spots he realized was his, not the *lion's,* blood.

Albert found his shotgun, opened the breach, and tried to look down the barrel. Evidently, when he threw the gun down, it had landed barrel first in the snow. The muzzle was jammed tight with a combination of mud and snow. He had no way of clearing it. He was utterly defenseless.

He turned his attention to Ringo's baying a few yards away and walked over to where he could see the dog. Ringo was lying flat on his belly in the tulles trying to dig his way into the end of a steel culvert nearly filled with ice. A dark space less than three inches high marked the escape route where the lion had evaded Ringo.

Utterly defeated and covered with bleeding wounds, Albert headed for home. The worst, it seemed, was yet to come. Somehow, he had to face Mrs. Albert and try to explain how somebody's sweet little house cat had shredded his new hat, gloves, parka, and insulated coveralls and left him covered with a plethora of stinging wounds.

Albert wiped a little stray goose down off his bleeding forehead and glanced across the seat.

Ringo was perched forward on the edge of the padded truck seat, anxiously studying the snowscape around them. The hound was looking for the next *lion*. The first encounter of the day had been a lot of fun but not very productive. He was anxious to get on with his day.

# Butch—A Tall Tale From Circleville

## *Tyler Brian Nelson*

Utah is a magnificent place. Its natural wonders are truly something to marvel at. The state is home to many wonderful peculiarities, like a lake that is difficult to sink in, the sweeping red rock in the south, and the alien world of the salt flats. Utah is no stranger to some interesting names and faces too. The American Moses, Brigham Young, led his people across the plains and established the state. The legendary humorist Mark Twain passed through and documented it in his memoirs. Even Philo Farnsworth, the pioneer of television, has his roots among the sagebrush.

However, there is one person with a history tied to Utah that you might not know. His name was Robert Leroy Parker. You might know him better as the famous outlaw Butch Cassidy. His early years were spent around the small town of Circleville. With a population of just over half a grand, you blink, and you'll miss it. If you're ever down that way, it's worth a stop because there you'll get to see the homestead of one of the most lawless men that ever lived. You might hear some good stories too. It wasn't too long ago I made a pass through and caught a good one. It goes like this.

\*\*\*

The town of Circleville, Utah, has always been a good and respectable place. The folks who lived there worked hard, and they still do, for that matter. One fine Sunday morning many, many years ago, the town woke up, put on their best, and set off for church.

The men had on their finest shirts and hats all pressed and proper. The women swirled in their dresses and enjoyed the shade against the morning sun from their bonnets. The little boys had been scrubbed until they shone, and the little girls bounced brightly in their skirts.

Wagon wheels rumbled to a halt, the children squealed with joy at seeing their friends, women chatted happily, and men shook hands firmly. Old Brother Allen smiled brightly as he threw the doors open wide to admit the crowd. They flowed into the chapel and filled the pews up to the brim. At ten o'clock sharp, the bishop stepped to the pulpit, and a hush fell across the room.

"My dear brothers and sisters," he began, "it is a pleasure to welcome you out on this beautiful Sabbath morning. I thank the Lord for another blessed opportunity to meet and to worship! Before we formally begin this meeting, I would like to remind everyone of our picnic, which will take place tomorrow morning down on the banks of the Sevier River. Now we will open this meeting with a hymn, Now Let Us Rejoice."

The Widow Adams stepped to the stand, and with a power that belied her small frame, raised her hymnal and conducting baton aloft. She began to wave with vigor, and away they went.

*Now let us rejoice in the day of salvation.*

The doors at the back of the chapel swung open. The volume of the hymn faltered a bit as the congregation swung about to eye this unusual interruption.

*No longer as strangers on earth need we roam.*

The storekeeper, a great slab of a man named Jameson Halter, stepped in.

*Good tidings are sounding to us and each nation,*

His hair was disheveled, his shirt untucked, and his face red and sweaty, as though he had run a great distance at a fast pace.

*And shortly the hour of redemption will come!*

His eyes swung over the congregation like a wary bull, back and forth until he spotted his target. "Robert Parker!" he roared.

The quarry in question, a young boy on the front row, turned with his eyes wide.

"I'll teach you to steal from me again!" said Jameson.

As the peril girded up its anger and set towards the boy, he put a plan into motion. From his pocket, he pulled a beetle. It was a real prize, all red and black and shiny. He'd picked it up on his way to church when his mother wasn't looking. With a sigh, he parted with his beloved possession. He stood up and lobbed it into the midst of a group of ladies on the fourth row. Robert had never heard anyone make such a fuss about a bug. Screeching and hollering, they scrambled away from the critter and into the aisle. Poor Jameson was swept away in a storm of frantic petticoats and stockings.

The congregation was well and truly divided at this point. The men chuckled as they watched the carnage, the pious tried to keep singing, and the fearful shrieks rose above it all. The Widow Adams kept up her conducting like she was personally orchestrating the pandemonium. Robert, proud of the proper ruckus he had caused, scampered down the aisle, across the now empty pew, and out an open window.

**\*\*\***

The minute the last amen had been pronounced, the young boys of Circleville went in search of Robert. They found him down by the pond; cap pulled low over his eyes and a fishing rod in hand.

"Ho, Bob!" they called out.

He peeked out from under his cap.

"Ho, boys!"

They circled up around Robert. "You had some quick thinking to get out of there!" said one of them. "Jameson was piping mad!"

"Don't know what he was fussing about," said Robert, "all I *did* was borrow a bit of line."

"He was mighty mad about you 'borrowing'," said another boy. "He got talking to your momma, and even the sheriff was in town to hear it! Says he's gonna give you a real good hiding!"

Robert let his hat slide back down over his eyes. "Maybe I ain't going back then."

The group of boys looked at each other and shrugged. "Suit yourself, we're off to supper!"

The boys scampered off to their respective destinations, and Robert began to think. Maybe it was time to move on. This town was small; he'd be found soon. Besides, he was tired of catching heat for doing the things a proper boy should do, like fishing and adventuring. He checked his pockets for supplies. A pocket knife, a lucky penny, and some yarn. Material enough for a man to strike out on his own. Robert stood up and dusted off his pants. With one last look back at the town, he slung his fishing rod over his shoulder and set off down the valley.

***

When Robert reached the southern mouth of Circle Valley, the sun began to set, and he decided to make camp. He climbed up a nearby ridge to survey the land. From the top, he could see most of the valley. Down the slope, about a quarter-mile further south, he could see a campfire flickering. Visitors, family and friends and such, were not uncommon in the valley, so he decided to investigate. Keeping low down in the sagebrush, he set off towards the fire.

As he crept closer, he could see two men squatting around the fire. They both had tin cups of stew and were slurping noisily. One was long and lanky, with sideburns that ended far too late down his face and pants that ended far too soon up his legs. The other was short and stout, borderline pudgy around his equator. His eyes glittered black above his stew-stained beard. Shiny pistols hung on their belts, and the tall one had a satchel at his side.

Back in the shadows behind them, they had thrown a blanket over the sagebrush to act as a tent. Behind the makeshift tent were picketed two scraggly horses that matched the characteristics of their owners, one lean and the other hefty. The shorter man took a long swig of stew.

"Say, Jeb," he said with his mouth full, "toss me the satchel, will you?"

Jeb swished the stew in his can around. "What for?" he asked.

"Just want to count it again, that's all."

Jeb took a sip.

"But Willy, it's my turn to carry it today."

"I know that," said Willy, "I just want to count again!" What's the matter?"

Jeb shook his head. "Nothing."

Willy sighed. "I can't believe it, Jeb. After all, we have been through together, and you still don't trust me!"

"No, no!" Jeb stuttered, "I trust you, Willy, I do! I just-"

"Just what?" asked Willy.

"Oh, nothing."

"Then toss that satchel over here." Willy held out his hand.

With a grunt, Jeb picked up the satchel and swung it over to Willy. As he caught it, Robert heard the clink of gold coins. Willy opened it and chuckled.

"Woo-Whee!" he said, "three hundred dollars straight gold, and all mine!"

"All *ours*." Jeb reminded him.

"Of course, of course," said Willy, "and as soon as we get up to this next town, we are going to get us some more!"

Robert had seen enough. He knew these two were trouble, and he figured he better get back to town and warn the sheriff. He began to back away, but his foot found a dry branch.

CRACK!

Both men jumped to their feet with weapons drawn. Willy clutched the satchel tightly.

"Who's there?" yelled Willy, "Come out quick, or we start shooting!"

Robert didn't have much of a choice. He stepped out of the sagebrush with his hands held high.

Jeb lowered his gun. "It's just a boy."

"What are you doing creeping around in the sagebrush, boy?" Willy asked.

Robert had to think fast. "I was just coming up from the south to visit my cousins in Circleville, sir. I saw the fire and figured you might be fellow travelers. I didn't know you, though, so I wasn't sure."

"Where you say you're headed, boy?"

"Circleville, sir."

"That the next town up?"

"Yes, sir."

"And you know the town?" Willy asked.

"Sure, been there loads of times," Robert said.

Willy looked at Jeb then back at Robert. "I got some business to do at the bank there; you could show me where it is?" Willy asked.

"Yes, sir."

Willy lowered his gun. "Good. Tomorrow we'll go up together. Until then, come have a seat and have some stew."

Robert sat down by the fire. Jeb handed him a cup of stew. "What's your name, boy?" he asked.

Robert took a bit of stew. "Err, Butch sir."

"Butch?"

"Yes, sir, Butch."

Jeb squinted at Robert. "Alright, Butch. I'm Jeb. This here is Willy."

Robert looked at Willy, sat on the other side of the fire. "What's in the satchel, Mister?" asked Robert.

Willy flinched."Nothing!" he said, "just some trail supplies."

"Which I'm supposed to be holding," said Jeb.

"Right, but it's the end of the day. What do you say we call it a night I keep the satchel?"

"Oh, alright," grumbled Jeb.

"There's a good man! I do believe that it's my night under the tent, so I'll be off!

Willy crawled into the makeshift tent and dropped to the ground. His feet stuck out the opening. Jeb leaned against a log and closed his eyes. Within minutes a chorus of snores echoed back and forth from Jeb and the tent. Robert put down his cup. As he sat back and looked up at the stars, he started thinking again. He looked at the horses and smiled.

***

Jeb woke with a start. He rubbed his bleary eyes and looked around. Willy's toes stuck out the end of the tent. A cold trail of smoke wound its way up from the dying coals, and the horses slept soundly on their feet. Where the boy had been sleeping, the dirt was stamped down, but there was no boy.

"Willy!" Jeb hissed, "Willy! The boy is gone! We've got to find him! He might have snuck off and—" He stopped and stared with his mouth open. Robert came trotting back into camp, his line over his shoulder and a half dozen fish in hand. Willy stuck his head out of the tent.

"What's going on?" he slurred.

"Nothing," said Jeb, "where you been, Butch?"

Robert held out the fish. "I thought you might get hungry. I caught some fish for breakfast."

Jeb smiled. "Well, I'll be! I'll get the fire on, and we'll eat." He resurrected the deceased embers while Robert prepared the fish. Willy crawled out from cover and took a seat by the fire. He put the satchel in his lap.

"Tell me something about Circleville, boy."

Robert put the fish on a spit and held them over the fire. "Not much to tell. It's real small. The people are good enough, though I reckon the cows outnumber them."

"Is there a sheriff?"

"Yes, but he doesn't come by much. Spends his time out in the country, unless there's trouble."

Willy beamed and nodded. "Let's eat and get on the road.

Robert passed around the fish. They ate in silence. When they all finished up, Willy clapped his hands. He had a nasty twinkle in his eye.

"Off we go!" he said.

*** 

The ride to Circleville took most of the morning. Robert rode with Jeb, swaying back and forth as the dusty horses plodded along, heads low. When the town came into view, the sun was high in the sky. As they passed an old, dilapidated barn, Willy reined his horse in.

"Who owns this barn?" he asked.

"I don't know, mister. It's been years and years since anybody has used it."

"Perfect," Willy said, "This satchel is weighing me down. I think I'll just hide it here for now and pick it up on the way out of town." Willy pried open the doors and placed the satchel under a pile of old planks. When he felt satisfied that the satchel wouldn't be disturbed, they continued to town. As they rode in, the place seemed deserted. Their only greeter was a dusty dog napping in the shade of a tree and a lone tumbleweed rolling by. Windows were shuttered, doors closed, and it was dead silent.

Jeb looked about with unease.

"Where is everyone?" he asked.

Willy and Jeb looked at Robert.

"Oh, that's right, I reckon they're all out at the picnic on the river. Sorry, Mister Willy, they won't be back until suppertime, I reckon, and the bank will be closed."

Willy smiled.

"Should be a clean break then— er, that is we're in a bit of a hurry to get our business done, Butch. We've got to get a move on. I say we'll just drop in and do our business and leave them a note, eh Jeb?"

Jeb didn't seem so sure.

"How'd you know about this picnic Butch?"

"My cousins sent me a letter about it. I'm supposed to meet them out there."

"Don't you worry about that right now, show us the bank boy!" Willy said.

Robert led them down the street to the bank. It sat a block west of the center of the city. It was a two-story affair, with a sturdy door and barred up windows. Robert climbed the steps and tried the door.

"Locked!" he called.

Willy came up the steps. "Out of my way!" He tried the door handle, rattled it back and forth, then put his shoulder into the door. It didn't budge.

"Blast!"

Robert scratched his head. "There might be another way in. Sometimes Mr. Jenkins likes to leave his office window open. Gets mighty stuffy in the summer."

"Where's this office at?" asked Willy.

"Round back."

"Show me."

Robert led them around the back of the bank. Sure enough, the middle window on the second floor was wide open. Jeb looked at Robert.

"You know a lot about this place for just visiting, Butch," he said.

Robert shrugged. "Been up here for a visit every summer, that's all."

"I don't know, seems a bit fishy to me. Willy, you—"

"Oh, forget about it, Jeb!" said Willy, "Butch here is helping us out. Now give me a leg up!"

Jeb got in position under the window. He cupped his hands, and Willy put his foot in them. He put his hand on Jeb's shoulder for balance.

"Alright, on three. One! Two! Three!" Willy jumped up, and with Jeb's added lift, he was able to catch the window sill with his fingertips. With considerable effort, he managed to haul himself through the window. After a few seconds, his cursing turned to whoops of joy.

"Jeb! The fool left his safe open! Bag of money right here!" Jeb drew his gun and turned to face Robert.

"Now see here Butch—"

But Robert was gone.

"Willy!" Jeb yelled. "He's gone!"

"You said that last time!" came the reply from the window.

"He's really gone this time! We got to go! He might have gone after the sheriff!"

Willy appeared at the window with a bulging money bag.

"Here! Take it!" He tossed the bag to the ground. It landed with a dull clatter. Jeb frowned.

"That don't sound like gold coins."

As he reached for the bag, a shot rang out. A sheriff and a pair of deputies appeared around the corner of the bank.

"Hold it right there!" the sheriff said, "That doesn't belong to you!"

Jeb drew his pistol and fired. The sheriff and his deputies ducked behind the bank.

"It's mine now!" cried Willy as he dropped from the window. The sheriff stuck his head out, and Willy fired at him.

"Jeb! Grab the bag, and let's go!"

Jeb snatched up the bag, and they ran for their horses. They mounted and set for the edge of town at full gallop. Hot on their trail came the sheriff and the deputies. They rode hard, spurring their horses faster and faster until they neared the old barn where they had left the satchel. To their surprise, Robert stood on the side of the road holding it. Willy drew his gun.

"Give it here, boy!"

"No problem, Willy! Here ya go!"

As they rode up, Robert tossed the satchel to Willy. "You better hurry! Here comes that sheriff!" said Robert.

BANG!

Another shot rang out. With a whoop and a holler, Willy and Jeb spurred their horses away. As the sheriff and the deputies came riding up, the sheriff reined in his horse.

"Keep them on their heels, boys!" he called out. He got off his horse and trotted over to Robert. "Well, Robert, did it work?"

Robert chuckled. "Like a charm!" He ran into the barn and came back with a burlap sack. He opened it, and the sheriff looked in. Three hundred dollars' worth of gold coins shimmered inside. The sheriff laughed.

"Well, I'll be! Robert, when you woke up Jenkins and me last night, I thought you were weaving us a yarn. But it worked! Those two will be halfway to Mexico before they realize all they made off with is rocks! That was a mighty slick idea, leaving the window and the safe open and swapping the money. I think I'll have to keep an eye on you. Soon enough, you'll be outsmarting the lot of us!

Robert just smiled and shrugged.

***

The next morning, when Jameson Halter opened his store, he found a note and a pile of gold coins sitting on his counter. The note read:

# Utah's Special Blend

*For all the goods and the misdeeds of Robert Parker. - Butch*

# Rodeo Scoring for Beginners

## *Don Miles*

Some of you may be confused by the scoring and rules as you watch rodeos, especially if you are new to the sport. I will try to explain some of the finer, often little-known rules and scoring procedures, like how a cowboy can get a perfect score on a ride, and I will throw in some subtleties about performing in the different events. This explanation should help you enjoy the rodeo more, perhaps even impress those around you, and certainly help you know what to watch for and what to laugh at.

Before the rodeo begins, many riders will walk, trot, and lope horses all over the arena to warm them up for the calf ropers, steer wrestlers, barrel racers, pickup men, and judges. This activity is not a scored event, and these riders are seldom in the rodeo itself; they are often the cowboys' and cowgirls' kids and the kids' friends. These kids can usually warm up the horses without being thrown or trampled on and thus experience a positive and fun introduction to rodeo. For the kids who go on to compete, the warmup may be the only positive and fun memories they have of the sport.

Some of the horses in this warmup are not in the rodeo either; they were brought by people who have more sense than to compete. These people bring horses to exercise them in a safe place. They bring their kids to ride them in a nice, fenced, plowed arena (which also has an ambulance standing by should the horse not be as well broke as the owner thinks).

The next segment of the rodeo is the Grand Entry. Unlike Hollywood events, no score is awarded for a grand entry in rodeo. In this event, the rodeo owner demonstrates that he can actually ride a horse, though he always rides an extremely tame, gentle one (like Hollywood stars do). And he never rides around the arena at full gallop like other riders. The owner gets no points, and correctly so, for his performance.

Also, during the Grand Entry, pretty girls show that they can ride horses with a flag in one hand, even though their horses detest flags and often try to jump and buck around the arena because of them. The girls get no score for their efforts, though incorrectly so, because some may exhibit the best bucking horse ride of the night.

Various other people are introduced in the Grand Entry, too, like the rodeo judge (the referee). At rodeos, no one boos the judge, mainly because no one knows how he figures the scoring. Let me explain how the judge scores the riding events: the bareback, saddle bronc, and bull riding.

Bareback riding, the event right after the Grand Entry, is the first one in which scores are kept. The rider must sit on the bare back of the horse, with no saddle to help hold him on or for padding as the horse jumps. The rider holds onto a bareback rigging (pronounced riggin', and if you pronounce it rigging, some cowboys will not understand you, others will think you mean ropes for ships and such, but the ones who can spell may figure out what you meant, but they will never trust you and will think you are a tin-horn or are putting on airs).

The best bareback score, in this event, the highest score that can be given is 100 points, 50 for the horse, and 50 for the rider. Total scores in the 60s or 70s are common. Scores in the 80s are good. Scores in the 90s are almost unheard of. If the cowboy is bucked off before the buzzer goes off after 8 seconds, he gets no score. Neither does the horse get a score, even though the horse won.

A rider must spur the horse on the first jump out of the chute according to current rules. (When I was young, they had to spur for three jumps.) If he fails to spur correctly on that first jump, he gets no score. If a rider spurs hard, flailing his legs at the front shoulders of the horse like a bee does his stinger to protect the honey, he may get 40 points. If the horse jumps high, lands hard, and kicks his hind legs high, twisting and turning in difficult rhythms, he may get 40 points.

Such action from horse and rider would make a difficult ride and achieve a total score of 80.

For a cowboy to get 100, the horse would have to buck hard enough to kick all four horseshoes off (if he has any, whether nailed to his hooves or glued on), bounce the cowboy 10 feet in the air between kicks, and scare the first three rows of spectators out of their seats.

The cowboy would have to stay aboard through all of this, spur the entire time, and eat a sack lunch nonchalantly with his free hand, making sure not to touch the horse with that free hand or any part of the lunch, or he will be disqualified. A cowboy should not eat anything with ketchup, however, because if any slopped onto his clothes or the horse, the judge might deem the red splotches as blood and dock the rider or horse for needless bleeding.

Saddle bronc riding is similar to bareback riding, but in this event, the rider has the advantage of a saddle. The person who made up this event decided that the saddle was almost cheating, so saddle bronc riders can only hold a rope on the horse's halter. Saddle bronc riders cannot touch any part of the saddle or horse with either hand during the ride, or they lose points.

Again the horse and rider get 50 points each for a total of 100, with fantastic scores being in the 90s. Since the saddle is such a significant advantage (?) to the cowboy, to get a 100, the horse would have to jump the arena fence and buck up through the bleachers, not only missing all spectators but also not spilling a single drink or overturning a single paper container of popcorn.

The cowboy has a tougher job. He must spur the first jump out of the chute (the same as a bareback rider), and pick up his wife or girlfriend from a bleacher, and then balance her in his free hand, being careful not to bruise her from the jarring of the horse bucking or his grip on her waist.

With the other hand, the cowboy holds the rope attached to the horse's halter. However, he must undo the rope from the halter, tie a honda (pronounced "hondue" by all the cowboys I know) in one end, and perform rope tricks for the remaining seconds of the ride.

For the last rope trick, he must lasso a light post on top of the grandstands, cut a seat from a board in the grandstand bleachers (using his teeth as the saw if he cannot karate chop it to proportion), make a swing for his wife or girlfriend from the rope and board, set her in it without harming her, and then gently push her in the swing as he finishes the ride.

Many cowboys who ride bareback and saddle bronc don't get off immediately after the buzzer sounds that signals the cowboy completed a successful ride. They ride around the arena, waiting for the pickup men to ride alongside the bucking horse to help them dismount. Pickup men do not come in padded trucks to make safe, Hollywood rescues.

These fellows ride up on horses (which <u>are</u> well broke) and lope alongside the bucking bronc so the cowboy can climb on or roll across the pickup man's horse and jump or fall to the ground. Some of these landings seem no better than if the cowboy had climbed, rolled, or simply fallen off the bucking horse in the first place, but some are incredibly graceful and beautiful landings. The graceful or beautiful landings get no more points than a crash landing, however.

Once the cowboy is on the ground, safely or not, the pickup men remove the bucking breeching (pronounced "britchen"), the strap wrapped around the horse's flanks that makes him buck. Finally, the pickup men remove the horse from the arena by coaxing, trickery, or force. The pickup men get no score. (Don't blame me for rules that seem unfair to you. I didn't make them.)

Bull riding is the last event and is considered, by all bull riders and most other folks, to be the most difficult. Again the scores are 50 for the bull and 50 for the rider, totaling 100. <u>Any</u> score here for the cowboy is a miracle, but cowboys want scores totaling above 90.

Rodeo bulls have been specially bred to make them challenging to ride. The skin on any bull is loose, but centuries ago, rodeo owners crossed their bulls, in some evolutionary enhancing way, with owls since people from that era thought those birds could actually turn their heads all the way around. From this cross, the rodeo bulls inherited skin that will slide all the way around their bodies. Rodeo bull skin can do this, though whether that came from the cross with the owls is not proven.

67

# Don Miles

As a cowboy sits on a bull's back in the chute, he can hold himself on top of the bull by holding onto the boards of the chute. But once the bull leaves the chute, the skin on his back automatically starts to slide the cowboy 3 to 4 feet down under the bull's belly. Cowboys start on the bull's back the first second, but some end up in the next second directly under the bull, looking out through his front legs. And the cowboy is sitting on the same patch of skin he started on, not slipping or sliding at all. And more amazingly, the skin on the bull's legs, shoulders, and hips has not slid.

With these facts in mind, a normal person would say that a cowboy who can stay on a bull for 8 seconds deserves an award. But not rodeo judges. If a bull whirls and spins so fast that even the spectators get dizzy, the bull could get 40 points, and if the cowboy stays on, he might get another 40, totaling 80.

To get a score of 50, the bull must buck and charge through the arena fence (wire ones are worth only 2 points, while concrete and rebar are worth 6), charge madly past the crowd into the horse trailers, smack the rider against all of them, jump or buck high enough that the cowboys touch overhead electrical wires and receives a shock at least once, and then must roll over the cowboy (twice if there is time).

During this activity, the cowboy must not remain idle or complacent. He must hook his spurs into the bull's skin and roll under the bull and back up the other side, like a boater in a kayak doing an Eskimo roll.

As the bull perforates the fence, the rider must pull a strand of wire from a regular fence, or a piece of rebar from a concrete fence, and fashion a hotdog stick from the metal. Then he must skewer a raw hotdog as he passes a refreshment stand, roast the hotdog in the bull's breath, and start to eat it before the 8 seconds of his ride are used up.

The rodeo clowns must do all they can to make the bull mad enough to kill the cowboy during the ride, but when the buzzer blows and the ride is over, they must then rescue the cowboy, so the bull does not skewer him on a horn and roast him. The clowns are mostly successful at this. (Successful or not, the clowns also get no score.)

Each bull rider wraps his hand onto the bull's back as tight as he can using a bull rope. To make his grip more secure, the rider rubs resin all over his glove and hand and the gripping area of the rope. Then he wraps the rope around the bull's body in such a way that if he dismounts on one side of the bull, the rope will disengage somewhat easily, and he is released. If he dismounts on the other side, the rope will bind and not release.

If this happens, then the clowns have to somehow grab the rider's arm and jerk up hard enough to get the binding rope to release the stuck hand, all while the cowboy at this point is often dangling and bouncing helplessly on the bull's side. Any rider caught like this will usually have that arm dislocated or broken, at times in several places, which on the bright side can make jerking up on the arm easier for the clowns as they try to free the rider.

Eskimo rolls are easier to perform if riders roll in the direction that binds the rope tighter. If the cowboy rolls the other way, his hand may slip out of the rope underneath the bull, allowing the animal to either step on him or embed his head into the wire or cement of the fence, either of which could force the rider to miss his date to the dance that night.

As you can see, rodeo cowboys, especially bull riders, need tremendous strength to compete successfully. Athletes in many sports turn to steroids for superhuman strength. However, steroids don't help rodeo athletes, especially bull riders, because they weaken ligaments that attach bones to muscles. If you think 500–600 pounds of dead iron weights will rip weakened ligaments from the bones of a pro weightlifter, think what 2,000 pounds of live, often disgruntled bull can do to rip ligaments from bone on a cowboy. Bulls sometimes succeed at this even when cowboys don't take steroids.

These riding events are the only ones, thankfully, that require scoring by the judges. The other events are timed, with the fastest time taking first place. Beyond enjoying the simple race, however, you should know some subtleties that influence the race outcome. Barrel racing, for example, seems simple to the uneducated viewer, but the running horse makes subtle changes to his leg movement. The object of this race is plain enough. Cowgirls lope their horses in a cloverleaf

Don Miles

pattern around 3 barrels in the arena and the one who does so the fastest wins.

Each horse lopes to the first barrel with his best foot forward, so to speak. Horses run all gaits by putting one foot down first naturally. But the cloverleaf pattern of the barrel race makes them turn around the barrels in different directions. The subtlety occurs en route to the second barrel. Just as a good basketball player must learn to dribble with both hands, a good barrel racing horse must learn to run with either foot forward. Thus the horse lopes around the first barrel with one foot forward, but en route to the second barrel, if he is a good barrel racer, he actually takes one step in which he switches his front feet and puts the other foot forward. You can see him do this if you watch closely. Very closely.

If you attend a rodeo in an indoor arena with a camera, instant replay, and slow motion, watch for the stride when the horse switches his front feet. You still may not see it because the camera operator will likely not know what to watch for and will not make it easy to see. You seldom have that experience watching football or basketball replays.

All horses do not switch their legs, but the fastest ones always do. The horse needs to have the correct foot hit the ground next to the barrel. That proper foot placement puts the horse slightly farther from the barrel, so he has less chance of knocking the barrel over and thus receiving five penalty seconds added to the score for each barrel knocked over.

Bulldogging is another event that seems easy. Two cowboys lope their horses alongside a steer, one on each side. Then one leans down from his horse, grabs the running steer's horns, slides out of the saddle, drops to the ground, stops himself and the steer from running forward, and twists the steer's head until he falls over, ending with all 4 feet in the air.

To illustrate how easy this event is, comparing it to football will help. In football, 250 to 350-pound offensive linemen try to block 250 to 350-pound defensive linemen from tackling the smaller 200 to 260-pound running back with the ball. The linebackers may need to make the tackle, and they weigh 200 to 260-pounds as well. All of these athletes have pads and helmets to help protect them from injury. Each play can take as long as needed to make all of this happen. Football players do not have to flip the running back until both feet are in the air. Simply touching any part of his body besides his foot or hand to the ground is sufficient, or stopping forward progress.

Bulldogging is a lot simpler. A man who weighs 150 to 250-pounds rides his horse, from a standing start, up alongside the steer, that weighs 600 to 800-pounds. The steer is usually running close to or at full speed when the cowboy catches him because the bulldogger has to give the steer a head start. And rodeo rules don't assume the cowboy will be fair or honest. Nor do the rules allow for one false start, as track athletes get.

The bulldogger starts his run in a chute behind the chute that the steer is released from, and the cowboy's chute has a rope (called a barrier) stretched across the front with a string in it. If the cowboys starts his horse too soon and hits the barrier before the steer runs far enough for his head start, his horse will break that string. Then the cowboy has a penalty, 5 seconds, added to his time.

Once the cowboy and his horse catch the running steer, the bulldogger drops from his running horse onto the head of the steer, grabbing the horns for handles, stops the steer from running, and twists his head to make him fall over. All 4 feet must be off the ground in the air before the time stops. Some cowboys have done this in 3 to 4 seconds. 5 seconds is a good time. And the cowboy gets no protective clothing. If he falls on the steer's horns, or if the steer impales him on his horns, the cowboy will just miss the rest of the rodeo and likely the dance.

Calf roping also appears simple enough. A cowboy on a horse chases a running calf, ropes it, gets off the horse, runs to the calf, and ties it up as fast as he can. The fastest time wins. Calf ropers have the same barrier in front of their horses and the same penalty if they don't give the calf a big enough head start. The event is also complicated by something the crowd often doesn't feel—a 20 to 30-mph wind. Even when there is no wind at the rodeo, especially in indoor arenas, the ropers still have to throw their ropes into a 20 to

30-mph wind because the horse runs that fast to catch up to the darting calf.

The task of throwing the calf down and tying him is made easier than bulldogging because it only weighs 250 to 450 pounds, while calf ropers often weigh 125 to 250 pounds. The clincher is the cowboy has to do this in his cowboy boots. I do not know if the rules require him to, but getting football cleats out of stirrups on a saddle could take 30 seconds alone, and good ropers finish the event in less than 10.

After the calf is tied, the judge counts off 6 seconds in his head before the score is official. If the calf struggles free and gets up during the 6 seconds, the roper gets no score. While most people count "one thousand one, one thousand two," rodeo judges have a shorter method: "111,111 one, 111,111 two."

In team roping, another event where subtleties are hard to see, two cowboys rope a long-horned steer, again with the fastest time winning, and also with the barrier penalty if the steer does not get a big enough head start. The first cowboy ropes the steer by the horns. If he catches him by the neck or head, the judge adds seconds to his time as a penalty. The second cowboy ropes the hind legs, or the "heels." If he misses, they get no score. If he catches only one leg, the judge adds seconds to their score.

The first roper uses a standard overhand throw to catch the horns. The second roper may use a trick in throwing his loop under the steer's belly at the heels. Some cowboys flip their wrist forward as they let go of the loop. By doing this, the top of the loop flips down very hard onto the ground in front of the steer's legs, and the bottom of the loop flips very hard against the steer's hind legs. Since the first roper is pulling the steer forward, the steer steps over the top of the loop, which is now on the ground, and the steer steps into the loop, because the bottom of the loop is smacked tight against his legs. Once both legs move forward into the loop, the second cowboy must pull the loop tight around both legs, catching them both in the loop before the steer can step forward enough to get one or both feet out. The ropers both pull their ropes tight, and the judge signals the catch is complete. Good times are under 10 seconds.

If you mention any or all of this detail loud enough that people around you can hear you at the next rodeo you attend, and if you wear Justin or Tony Lama boots, Wranglers, a western belt with a large buckle, a western shirt, and a Stetson, people may think you are a real cowboy—which may not be to your advantage.

They may ask you to help break a horse, help shovel out their trailer or semi, help load the horses or other farm animals, help vaccinate, dehorn, and brand their animals, help clean barns and pens, and so on. If you are not ready to work that hard or shovel that much manure (pronounced manore, though you may hear one syllable pronunciations as well), you might want to just remain silent with all this knowledge.

# How I Corrupted an Entire Utah Town

## *Monique Berish*

I've moved a lot.

All over the country, actually.

I started out in New Jersey then moved to New Mexico as a teen. Since then, I've been all over the west from Anchorage to San Diego and back. I settled in Utah about five years ago after spending the better part of my life driving through it on my way somewhere else.

Every new place requires a period of acclimation, which includes testing out the local eateries. Since my roots are in New Jersey, bakeries and hole-in-the-wall diners are favorites, but I'm open to trying anything, restaurant, deli, even a taco truck. I also fancy myself a bit of a foodie. Couple that with my love for writing and a decent following on social media and, ta-da meet the newest, local, amateur reviewer.

Prior to moving here, every culinary experience in Utah was dismal at best and downright abominable at worst. I once ate a pizza here that was probably given to prisoners as a form of torture. I complained to friends, and someone told me I really needed to try the buffets. I'm sure they weren't actually trying to kill me. Probably just a coincidence. I had faith that it was simply bad luck, and these experiences were not representative of the state as a whole. I was not wrong. Utah came through

Utah was no different from any of the other places I'd ravaged in my search for the perfect local food joint. I'd start my investigation with Google, then Yelp, and finally, local friends for confirmation. My journey brought me to the BEST BREAKFAST IN THE

STATE at Penny Ann's Cafe (better known as the PAC), Gourmandise, (stuffed avocado anyone?) and of course The Garage on Beck for literally the best fried funeral potatoes I've ever had. They were the ONLY fried funeral potatoes I've ever had, but trust me; all others would pale in comparison. I know this because sometimes when it comes to food, it's more of an emotion than a taste. And those potatoes caressed my soul.

When I ran out of places I'd searched on my own, I'd take to social media and have others give recommendations. Each time I indulged in a new culinary delight, I'd share my thoughts and write up a thorough review. It's always interesting to me what people consider "good food" in their local area—especially in ultra-conservative Utah, where pepper is considered "spicy."

The posts on social media were great fun. I loved hearing people argue for or against my decisions about a certain place or dish, with feigned aggression and puffed-up statements that would even devolve into clever insults. I was always pro-insult as long as it was clever. You can call me a name, but make it creative. If you're just going to dredge up tired old cuss words or insults that have made the rounds for years, then I don't have time to engage. A good intelligent insult goes a long way with how much I respect a person. That's probably the Jersey in my DNA talking.

Maybe it was karma from all that social media arguing, but much to my horror, shortly after moving here, I discovered I had issues with gluten. Up until that point in my life, my entire diet was one long gluten train of pastas, breads, and intestinally explosive sauces. My entire identity as a foodie was plucked like a used bay leaf from grandma's stew and tossed into the nearest trash bin. However, my health demanded I make drastic changes to my lifestyle, including a low carb diet (the horror!) and increased time dedicated to losing my will to live. Or, as others like to call it, going to the gym.

I suspect my issues with gluten were always there. I have had stomach problems since I was a kid. However, as I got older, things began to progress in ways that were getting serious. I didn't make the connection to gluten until I tried a keto diet. Within a few short weeks, every health problem I had developed disappeared. Even then,

I was too dense to make the connection fully, and it wasn't until I went off my diet and started eating gluten again that I realized it was the culprit of all my gastric ills. I mean, why couldn't it just be a heart attack? Or Covid or anything else? Why gluten? The universe, in its ironic interventions, had to be to blame.

The foodie...gluten-free.

After several months of not getting out of bed–because why? I decided that it was going to be okay. ...Because I truly did feel better and I was a strong independent woman who wasn't going to let a cardboard-flavored, gluten-free pizza take me down.

Mostly.

Probably.

When my pity party ended, I decided that instead of eating out, I would cook at home. I started reviewing low carb recipes. Counting carbs and eliminating as much gluten as possible while still creating food worth eating was my focus.

And there were some happy endings.

I discovered bread cheese, almond flour bagels, and keto ice cream. However, as with most things, I settled into a pattern and became bored with the same options. For instance, I had also cut out all soda and refined sugars. Drinking water was getting old. I missed the fizz of soda. And even though diet soda was an option, I knew that it still wasn't good for me. I tried things like La Croix through a grimace and a forced swallow. No thanks. What was left?

About a year or so into my foray with healthy, I found these amazing drinks called "Neuro" drinks. They were 35 calories and had different functions. Neuro Sonic had a blast of caffeine and got your day going. Neuro Sleep had 5 mg of melatonin and was great for the occasional sleepless nights. They also had drinks to boost immunity and more. However, Neuro is not paying me for this commercial, so I'll quit here. Just know there were lots of options with this line.

I fell in love with them. I'd been buying these drinks pretty faithfully when I stumbled on their website and discovered there were EVEN MORE that I'd never tried. I went on Amazon and loaded up. After ordering from Amazon a few times, I decided it would be a lot more convenient if I could just get my local Harmon's to carry them, so I contacted the purchasing manager and introduced him to some of the lines he was not carrying. This was my first attempt at trying to influence the local culture to accommodate my particular tastes. I should have known this would not go well. Adapt, don't make waves. That's always been my motto.

Here's where it gets tricky. I specifically tried to emphasize that they should only add the Neuro Trim line because when I was investigating the other lines offered, I discovered one of them was a sexual performance enhancer called Neuro Gasm (hehe). So I made my case for the Neuro Trim and left it at that, never mentioning the Gasm line.

About a week or so later, I walked into Harmon's, and it quickly became apparent that the manager had done some further research, but maybe not as much as he should have. Or perhaps he did plenty of research. Who am I to judge. You do you, Harmon's ordering guy. Because there, at the end cap, on full display, at your local Harmon's, in ultra-conservative Utah, were the sexual enhancement Neuros. Yanno, right next to the apples in the produce aisle. HAPPY MARRIAGES FOR EVERYONE TONIGHT!

Yes, I bought five. Don't judge.

It's been three years now since I've repented of my gluten ways. I can't say I love it. I don't. I still cheat. The PAC pancakes still call to me. At night my soul longs for the starchy caress of fried funeral potatoes. I've tried reviewing some of my favorite low carb, keto dishes, but nobody wants to hear about that. Nobody. And I can't blame them. How am I supposed to argue the merits of gluten-free, sugar-free, keto muffins when there are fresh croissants at Gourmandise? My review days are over. But all is not lost. After all, I managed to corrupt an entire Utah town by introducing sexual enhancement drinks into their local grocery store. Next up, CBD bakery sections…

# Utah's Urban Assault Vehicle

## *Steve Odenthal*

U tah is famous for a variety of things and infamous for a few more. Justified or not, one thing that the beehive state seems to be world-renown for is kids. There's a lot of them. Take a look around, you will find them everywhere. Tall ones, short ones, they come in all sorts of configurations, running amuck in the malls and suburban backyards of most every city or town. They seem to be the state's renewable resource that is constant and not endangered. Must be something in the water. I can recall some years ago, a beverage company laying claim to a special ingredient they called "rocky mountain spring water," but I doubt that has a connection to the number of kids per household. Well, maybe dependent on the household. Perhaps a study is in order here. The jury is still out.

When you deal with tribes this big, it can be a challenge logistically to bring the brood to an event or activity, especially when family economics dictate rationed gasoline and bench seats to accommodate all. Any trip more than around the corner brings with it a chorus of rants and chants like: "He's in my space!" "She breathed my air!" "Are we there yet?" "Don't we have 11 kids? Where's Tommy?"

Questions like these are typical for Utah families. They are why you see many larger vehicles with cute depictions of stick-figure clans decorating the back window of Chevy Suburbans and family vans all up and down the state's roads. Those caricatures are not merely to show the family's lighter side and creativity, but the images have a functional purpose. If you are observant and catch a Utah family leaving a restaurant, amusement park, or special event, you might notice the designated driver supervising the loading of his or her family, making sure none have strayed. They do this by standing just off the driver-side rear panel, behind the side door, where they can count and compare the on-boarding to the depiction, ensuring that, indeed, Tommy is still with them.

You might have caught the term I used—designated driver. Outside of Utah, you hear that term describing a person who ensures a good outcome and safe travel home after a night of frivolity, sometimes involving the previously mentioned "rocky mountain spring water" or other intoxicants. But that is not what my word choice represents here. No. The designated driver in a Utah family van is the one parent who can best not be driven insane by the other drivers on the road while tuning out the rants and chants within the vehicle. That assignment is much more challenging than it sounds on paper. A lot of little qualities and talents are needed to assume the role. For instance, a rugged and sturdy back of the head is highly desirable for any Utah family chauffeur, as tennis shoes are known to be kicked off regularly at the mile six marker. Once off, any sneaker becomes a potential projectile, and by milepost ten, someone in the backseat has decided the shoe is a football, and the driver's ears make for perfect goalposts. That someone is usually Tommy. To add insult to injury, if the family is into soccer rather than the NFL, the competition between the kids as to who can hold the longest "GOOOOOOOOOOAAAAAALLLLLL!" can get real old fast.

The Utah designated driver is only good for so many miles and/or hours, dependent upon how many low-top projectiles have been bounced against their noggin. A sure sign it is time to change drivers is when, after the latest assault, the driver yells, "THAT'S IT!" and throws Tommy's shoe out the window. I have come under direct attack from on-coming vehicles three separate times by flying tennis shoes on Utah roads. You know it happens, but you never expect it to happen to you. It can shake you up pretty good to be traveling 75 miles per hour and have a sneaker bounce off your windshield or skim across your head if the top is down on the convertible. I will say most Utah residents are reasonably polite, so you occasionally hear someone yell, "Sorry!" as they fly by you going the other direction. You can be sure that apology isn't coming from shoeless Tommy in the backseat; he's too busy giggling. Most likely, it was the next driver up who issued the windswept apology, foolishly thinking that they will be able to handle the chaos a little better than their predecessor when they take the wheel.

The sanity level of the driver seat occupant on a Utah family excursion has a direct correlation between vehicle length and the number of kids hauled (with or without Tommy.) In the good old days, Chevy Suburbans were *the* thing. Calculation of miles-per-gallon was not a consideration once a fourth child entered the toddler stage. Space. Space, the final frontier, was the all-important ingredient to ensure sanity for those weary parents in the front seat. You still would have just as many wars and skirmishes, but the shorter arms of children made it harder for them to span the distance to invade a rival's air-space. Oh. Sure, Tommy's shoes were still flying, but it took a lot more arm to launch a successful air-assault.

Suburbans were awesome. When you climbed down from one of those puppies, shut your door, and pumped your wallet into the gas tank, a designated driver would feel alive, or at least in a different zip-code. The noise stayed in the vehicle because those babies were built well and fully insulated. The 20-minutes it took to fill the tank felt like a mini-vacation from your vacation. By the time you climbed back into the driver's seat, you were ready to roll, plus the kids should have all been to the bathroom by then. Suburbans were the BEST and were nicknamed *Urban Assault Vehicles* in most young neighborhoods—they were everywhere.

Families could haul anything in them. Children were the most common commodity toted, but at times lumber, bags of cement, canoes, bikes, soccer teams, fully-inflated rafts, Christmas trees, and a host of other things routinely traveled the state in or on them without a UHP officer batting an eye. There was only one time that I recall a big deal being made by law enforcement during a more innovative use of a Suburban in Utah. Luckily, I know all the short story details, as I was the driver of said Suburban.

Skipping the backstory, I found myself directing a hilarious spoof called *Peter Pun* using a script and many props from the Off-Broadway Theatre in Salt Lake City. The production was to be staged 60 miles north of SLC at the Brigham City Fine Arts Center. One of my actors kindly lent his muscle and his Suburban to the cause, and the two of us filled the vehicle to its brim with everything that we would need to stage this great show. There was only one issue; we had filled the interior thoroughly; no nook or cranny was unfilled. But we did not have room for one last prop. That prop was integral to the story, so we had to figure something out. Then it hit us, "Hey, we still have the *top* of the vehicle to use. Problem solved!"

We lashed and strapped down our life-sized stage-prop and then set out to leave the downtown area, hoping to make quick time to the I-15 freeway so that we would miss the heaviest of commuter traffic heading north. We hadn't made it even three blocks in the city when an SLCPD cruiser pulled beside me, radio in hand, and started looking our vehicle over. We noticed the officer but reasoned we weren't in violation of any traffic rules, so it was safe to proceed. Within a block, another cruiser joined our entourage, this time on the passenger side. Again, no reds and blues, so we nervously moved on toward the freeway entrance. The second officer seemed quite interested as well, and it became apparent that we now had an escort out of town.

The two officers peeled off as our prop-mobile entered the on-ramp. We accelerated toward I-15 and merged with the go-home traffic. Merging at that time of day usually is a challenge as most drivers don't want to give up an inch of hard-earned space, but this day the commuters seemed quite willing to give us some room. In fact, a few cars may have been taking off-ramps they usually didn't once they caught sight of our Urban Assault Vehicle approaching from behind. We even noticed a few kids taking pictures of our vehicle as we passed them.

About five miles up the road, just past the Bountiful off-ramp, we spotted a UHP mustang with lights flashing on the side of the road. All traffic bogged down as we all put on our best driving manners and watched out for what might be an accident up ahead. We traveled on cautiously, passing the officer as he killed his lights and joined in with the traffic behind us. Slowly, he maneuvered his vehicle in and out of traffic until he was matching my legal speed just off my left flank, neither gaining nor giving ground. I hate when that happens, but at least he was not in my blind spot so that I could see him in my side mirror. I watched him pick up his radio; I could only guess what he was telling his dispatcher but figured it was about me. But then, the officer smiled. I saw it plain as day. He sped up beside me, popped his red lights for a second, merged a lane over to the left, and gave me a thumbs-up before speeding off further north. I proceeded on my way, feeling pretty good about things.

From that point on, I realized that our Urban Assault Vehicle was essentially the Grand Marshall entry of an unannounced parade. As we passed one city after the next, Layton, Roy, and then Ogden, at least one representative of law enforcement, served as an escort along our way back to Brigham City. Word had traveled fast through the crackling radios and broad grins of our finest in blue. It's a trip I will always remember. It's a shame little Tommy had to miss it. He loves watching police chases, and one way or another seems destined to be a participant someday. Maybe not. He probably would've been up on top lighting the fuse or inside throwing tennis shoes anyway.

Utah's Urban Assault Vehicle

# Dawn of a New Millennium

## *Tim Keller*

As per our annual tradition, January 1, 2000, found my small group of friends ringing in the New Year at the Crystal Springs Resort in the hills of Northern Utah. It was a memorable evening in more ways than one. Yes, it was the first night of the new millennium, but more importantly, we had finally managed to convince my friend Mark to join us.

Everyone else donned their swim trunks quickly and were already making the pilgrimage through the cold to the warmth of the pool. To prevent his escape, I waited patiently for Mark to get changed. Already he was carping from behind the door of the dressing slot, which was clearly filled to capacity.

"Look at this place," Mark grunted. "It's filthy! God only knows why I let you talk me into this."

"You'll feel better when we get outside," I soothed.

"Yeah, why's that?"

I was suddenly grateful we'd come at night. It wasn't so much that the resort was particularly unclean. But Crystal Springs boasts the highest mineral content of any hot spring in the world, which gives the water a slightly swampy hue.

"Too dark to see the filth," I said.

The door popped open to reveal my less-than-amused friend in a stylin pair of denim shorts, which were likewise filled to capacity.

"Not a word," Mark huffed as we walked into one of those crystal clear nights only extreme cold can bring about.

Mincing carefully to avoid the patches of ice that lined the pathway, we maneuvered through the darkness and settled at last into the steam-covered water.

Squeals of delight wafted across the resort. Seconds later, some teenagers half-ran, half-danced back to our pool.

"Oh, cool," I said. "The slide is open."

Mark snorted.

"What?"

"You couldn't get me down that thing on a dare," Mark growled.

"Why not?"

"Just couldn't, that's all."

"Wait, you've never been down a water slide, have you?"

No answer.

"How do you get to be thirty-five years old without ever going down a water slide?"

Mark shrugged defensively. "Lots of people haven't."

"Yeah, in Afghanistan."

I know it sounds silly—grown men arguing over a water slide—but that's the nature of our friendship. I remembered the day we met. I'd seen him around, of course, but we met at a training retreat where they made us play one of those ridiculous, time-wasting ice-breaker games corporate trainers are so fond of.

Our hostess smiled like a predatory kewpie doll. "Mark," she said, "I want you to tell Tim something about yourself. Something he didn't know before."

Mark furrowed his brow as though he were deep in thought. "You know," he said, "I've never liked you."

The room held its collective breath.

"That's all right," I said. "Who are you again?"

"Oh, come on," he pressed. "You know me, don't you?"

"Well, I know everyone calls you 'Mr. Clean.'"

"Oh," he huffed, "because I have OCD, right?"

"No, because you look like the guy on the bottle, but the OCD thing—that's interesting."

The tension broke, and a friendship was born. It's like that sometimes; two overbearing people collide and then connect.

Mark's response snapped me back to the pool.

"I spent my time on more intellectual pursuits, thank you."

This simple deflection told me all I needed to know. Mark was afraid. Hard to imagine a man the size of a tank being afraid, and—in fairness—he usually isn't. But with his OCD, given the right set of circumstances, Mark is the elephant terrorized by a mouse.

Just getting him to the pool, a non-chlorinated public pool, and in the dead of winter, was a Herculean task on both our parts, a reality that I should have accepted and been grateful for. I was—really except for, well, his "intellectual pursuits" comment. That was a mistake for which he had to pay.

"It's okay if you're afraid—"

"I don't see you on it," Mark snapped.

"At least I have done it," I reminded him. "I liked it, I was very good at it and, most amazingly of all, I didn't die."

"Well, you're too old now."

And the fight was on, escalating until the words "I dare you" were uttered. And suddenly, we were ten. See, the thing about guys is, regardless of how mature we seem, we never really grow up.

That's how, on the first day of the new millennium, my best friend Mark and I found ourselves side by side, huffing like a pair of locomotives up the tunneled stairs leading to the top of the water slide at Crystal Hot Springs Resort.

Steam rose from the warm water and sprayed from pipes along the walls to keep ice from forming on the steps. Kids raced around us as though we were merely monolithic obstacles placed there for their amusement. Their demented giggles wafted back through the steam, creating a distinctly creepy air.

When at last we reached the top, the argument began anew.

"Go ahead," I said.

"I'm not going first. You go."

As we stood deferring, a steady stream of teenagers cut around us to dive into the slide.

"You wanna go like them?" I asked. "They're going for speed, and they'll never wait for you. I, on the other hand, will."

The logic of my argument was unassailable, and so, a buoy released from its anchor, Mark drifted lazily into the darkness, steam rising from his body like smoke from a Viking funeral ship. I knew I was in for a long, cold wait.

And wait, I did, forever, really.

"Come on, mister, it's cold," the teens behind me protested. "He's far enough—please? Let us go first if you're scared."

That last statement roused a part of me I thought long dead.

*Scared? Mister? I'll show them scared. I'll show them, mister. I was blazing down water slides before these little shits were born.*

I grabbed the bar over the hydro tubes' gaping maw and swung into the slide like Tarzan from a vine.

I neglected to consider that, what served as a toy for kids (and adults of lesser size and greater maturity), becomes the watery equivalent of a suicidal bobsled run for people of "substance." The sensation of hurtling danger brought back my childhood. Never had I gone so fast; not for years had I felt this free. Yet through it all, I could hear an inarticulate something.

"Stop!" Mark's voice echoed into clarity. "I'm stuck."

And as often occurs just before a horrific accident, time slowed down.

"Stop, stop!" Mark screamed again as I whipped around the bend. "I'm stuck."

Now Mark is an intelligent man, brilliant even. In spite of his panic, I saw the realization in his eyes—his denim shorts anchored him to the slide like Velcro, and we were going to crash. Even so, he made a valiant effort to escape. Mark turned and paddled with both hands like a wounded seal on Shark Week.

For a moment, just one, I was hopeful. If Mark could get out of my way in the half-second he had remaining, whales could un-beach themselves, and penguins could fly. Heck, Nessie might even be real.

Alas, the laws of physics would not be denied. All I could do was coil my legs to my chest on impact, then hurl Mark into the darkness.

That's when I heard hoots and squeals and felt the rush of water from upstream. I realized that while I had waited patiently for Mark, the kids behind us gave no such consideration. I leaned back to accelerate, only to find Mark had run-aground again.

"Get your ass in the air!" I shouted. "Get your ass in the air!" My voice reverberated through the hydro-tube. "Heels and shoulder blades! Heels and shoulder blades! *Get your f\*\*\*ing ass in the —*"

Wham! The impact of a teenage body cut off my wind, and the effect of several behind him drove me ahead like a gunshot, straight into my bewildered friend. This time he did throw his ass in the air and blazed away like a scalded cat, but the staccato concussion of several bodies launched me as well, and yet again, I was closing in.

Mark looked back as we reached the end of the slide. He appeared to accept the inevitability that the moment he exited the slide, I'd land right on top of him.

However, when he dropped from sight, I threw my legs up, leaned backward, and somersaulted over him. Our combined water displacement triggered a tsunami that washed away the boys sitting on the edge of the pool.

Disheveled but otherwise unhurt, we made our way back to the therapy pool, the subject of many a curious glance.

# The Magical Wooing Water

## *DeAnne Mattix*

Spend any time in Utah around parents of adult children aging perilously out of prime marriageable age, and you will likely spot them finding a way-- sometimes not so subtly—to play matchmaker. It's rather like that urgency we feel to take care of slightly dented or expiring *best-used-before* canned goods. Things can get so desperate that sometimes extended family members and friends get roped into the project.

In my sophomore year in college, I shared a room with a girl named Robin. When she covered one wall with numerous eight by ten glossies of two guys, I assumed the pictures were of her boyfriends. I soon found out they were actually her two older (in Utah culture, *significantly* older) fraternal twin brothers. *Single*—as in *unmarried*— twin brothers. And when anyone entered our room, Robin immediately began to rhapsodize on the many fine qualities possessed by one or the other of them.

One afternoon when Robin was supposed to be in class, I decided to take a closer look at the collage on her wall. While Robin was a stunning redhead who had done some modeling in her earlier years, it appeared the good-looks gene had unfortunately been rather scant when the twins were conceived. They may have been adorable in their elementary school years, but they certainly seemed to have let self-care slide by a significant margin as they entered their thirties as two very sulky looking bachelors.

Ricky (I secretly nicknamed him *"Butch"*) seemed to be the very image of a perpetually disheveled garage mechanic. He wore his dirty blonde hair in a flat-top crewcut, apparently considered grease-covered white t-shirts the ultimate attire for all occasions, and sported quite the collection of scandalous tattoos. Rodney (I named him *"Slick"*), on the other hand, appeared to be a suit and tie kind of guy. Hollywood might have typecast him as a smooth used-car salesman. His dark, slicked-back hair and meticulously tended mustache seemed to yearn towards sophistication, but the scowl he wore in every picture somehow subtracted from the overall effect.

"Aren't they both *hotties?*" asked Robin, coming into the room with fast food. Apparently, she had cut class and taken herself out for lunch.

*Hotties....* hmmm. I struggled for a diplomatic response. "Well, I bet no one ever thinks they're identical twins."

If I'd thought Robin's well-rehearsed sisterly sales pitches felt vaguely like a marketing campaign, it was nothing to what lay just around the corner. It was only a couple of days later that she got a call from her parents in Arizona. They were planning a three-day weekend at the family cabin in southern Utah, and all Robin's roommates were invited—with all meals and mileage covered by Robin's parents!

Well, four of us roommates were more than willing to leave school behind and head out into the woods. It was while we were packing that Robin first mentioned the amazing spring water at the family cabin. Because her parents had been the first to purchase land in the small valley, they'd chosen a lot closest to a natural spring and had built a holding tank just up the hillside from the cabin.

"You've never tasted water like ours," Robin told us." It's crystal clear, right out of the spring."

Amazingly, the fact that the bachelor twins had *also* been invited to the cabin was never dropped into the conversation until we pulled up in front of the cozy little cabin. Then Robin enthusiastically "surprised us." All of us froze for just a second as we stepped into what was obviously a sophisticated trap.

Robin's parents were busy unloading their Jeep and arranging food for our first shared meal. I looked around curiously for Robin's brothers and soon saw them. *Butch* was stretched out comfortably in a hammock strung between a couple of pines. He had a boom box balanced across his considerable belly and appeared uninterested in packing in groceries or setting up camp. *Slick*, on the other hand, was already hard at work "camping"—he was wading in a nearby creek, gobbling up a large bag of Fritos and swatting at flies.

Meanwhile, the parents struggled with the heavy luggage and boxes of supplies. I tried not to show my dismay as my roommates and I rushed to help. Neither of the twins lifted a finger—in fact, other than tossing a few logs into the firepit, they didn't help out the entire weekend.

Robin's dad, Bob, waved hello. "C'mon, ladies! Come up here on the porch out of the heat. My wife, Ruth, is getting you some of our amazing spring water." Sure enough, Ruth appeared with a platter of camping cups filled to the brim. I had heard all about this water over and over on the drive down, but now it was time to check it out for myself.

It was plenty cold; I'll give it that. But as I raised the cup to my lips, I was almost certain it had a weird musky odor. Everyone else gulped theirs down, though, so I chalked it up to just tasting different than the city water I was used to.

My mother had once told me that the best way to judge a potential mate was to watch how he treated his mother. Over the next three days, we were treated to a spectacular array of disrespectful, coarse, and downright rude behaviors from the twins towards their parents—especially their mother. But Ruth didn't seem to mind at all. Instead, she scuttled around waiting upon her grown sons, making special adjustments to their meals and working herself to exhaustion to placate their constant whining.

Seemingly oblivious to the brazen impertinence of his sons, Bob kept busy tending to the Dutch ovens and plying us with cups full of the famous spring water. I couldn't figure out this family's obsession with their water! By day two, my other roommates had also detected a strange odor and taste in the water---a strangeness which Robin's family seemed to be oblivious to.

With only three days to work some kind of magic, the parents immediately set to work with their thinly disguised attempts to do some matchmaking. Every meal became a game of musical chairs as the benevolently smiling parents took turns trying to cozy up different girls by each bachelor in turn. All the while, the brothers took turns leering rather suggestively at us. Robin played her part with vigor, obviously hoping an engagement might be imminently announced. It was like the worst blind date in history, with nowhere for any of us to escape to.

The day we were to leave, my roomies and I started packing early. We eagerly volunteered to clean up the cabin site, roll-up sleeping bags, and pack the cars ---anything to get out of having to sit next to either twin and listen to their bragging or drink any more of the famous spring water. We didn't want to offend our hosts, but we'd had about all we could take of their sons, and the water by now was downright scary.

When the vehicles were loaded, Ruth came out one last time with the famous platter. We had skirted carefully around the water issue all morning, but now, lined up in front of our car, we had no way to get out of the Great Farewell Toast required before locking up the cabin.

With swelling pride, Bob raised his cup high and took a giant swig. Then his face changed.

"Ruth," he said. "Uh....do you think our water tastes a little...*off?*"

Obligingly, Ruth took her swig, dutifully followed by Robin and the bachelors.

The roomies and I stalled, holding our cups just out of range of our noses. Clearly, the water smelled more rank than ever. No way on earth were any of us were going to swallow another drop of it.

Bob swirled his cup thoughtfully and allowed himself another swallow.

"Boys?" he said to the twins. "Come with me. Let's check out the spring and the holding tank."

They weren't gone long.

*Butch* came ripping down the hill holding his stomach. "Gross!" he hollered.

*Slick* wasn't far behind. "That's disgusting!" he added.

Finally, Bob came shuffling slowly down the hill, shaking his head.

"Well?" Ruth asked. We were all anxiously waiting for the verdict.

Bob just seemed perplexed. "Shined my flashlight in the tank," he said. "Saw a couple glowing eyes in the water, so I poked a stick in there. Turns out, there's a dead raccoon floating in the tank. Pretty bloated up, so I don't know how long he's been in there."

Four cups of water were simultaneously dumped on the ground with amazing speed.

Bob continued. "I fished the dang thing out, so the water should be fine now."

When my roommates and I finally got back late that night to our own apartment, we all headed towards the kitchen and sucked down plenty of delicious normal-tasting city water.

"Guess the magical wooing water didn't work," one of my roommates whispered when Robin was out of the room.

"What do you mean?" I asked.

"Well, if it was supposed to help make us fall in love with those twins, it clearly failed!"

# Storing Your Year's Supply—In Your Couch

## *Don Miles*

If you are having trouble finding room enough to store a year's supply of food and clothes in your house, try using something you already have, namely your couch before you make expensive additions to your home or rent a storage unit. Couches are much cheaper, and they will actually hold more food and clothes.

I have always tried to have a year's supply of food ever since children started arriving from heaven to our family. Sometimes we have had an adequate supply, and other times we haven't had near so much.

But we have learned a few things about food storage, both from watching others store it and from doing it ourselves. These are some of the best tips we have picked up.

Some people use an entire room to store food and clothing, which, in effect, turns that room into a kind of store right there in their homes. Some people who live in mansions use more than one room, but they have to be careful when friends and neighbors drop-in, because at times, those folks can't always tell the difference between such a house and the local Target.

The friends start loading items into their baby stroller or a kid's wagon, and they get very upset when told the items are not for sale. This situation is exacerbated when the price tags are still on the items and are old enough to be much lower than current prices in stores. Some of these friends go so far as to threaten to never shop there again when forced to return items to the mansion. Imagine how embarrassed, not to mention threatened, the homeowner feels when this happens.

Other people that we know have stored food differently. Our friends who have more kids than food storage, and hence have no spare room, have built shelves or cupboards along a wall or two in a room, but they still use that room for other purposes. If you decide to use this approach, don't build the shelves in the living space of your biggest eater.

Some people have done that and found that the entire year's supply was consumed as midnight snacks in less than four months by the big eater, who showed no sign of eating less at regular meals or gaining weight while munching the year's worth of uncooked wheat, rice, noodles, and powdered milk.

If you decide to build a few shelves in a room for food storage, experience shows the best advantages accrue from constructing them in your master bedroom. This build, which could possibly turn into a full remodel, will force you to clean your room and move most if not all of the hoarded junk you have stacked against the walls into the garage. You can throw some of it out, of course, but only as a last resort.

Relocating the dusty hoard from bedroom walls to the garage will also force you to clean the garage, which will force you to relocate much of the garage treasures out into your shed. If you do not have a shed, this treasure moving could cause you to build one or buy one. If you cannot afford either approach, then you will be forced to rent a storage unit.

The main advantage of the storage unit is you won't need money for long. You simply stop paying the rent, and the storage managers will sell your junk at auction. You will be rid of it without the hassle of cleaning it for a garage sale, and you won't have to evaluate each item for pricing. You also won't have all that useless cash piled around the house from the sale, which could tempt you to repurchase your old items.

The best advantage of the storage unit managers selling your trash is that you won't know who bought it, and therefore you can't call them and offer to buy it all back.

Utah's Special Blend

The most overlooked advantage, a blessing really, of building food shelves in *your* room is that if you build the shelves in any other room, you will not feel forced to clean the room and then the garage and shed and so on. In a kid's room, for instance, you will just rearrange junk, moving it from one wall to another, to a closet, to the top of a dresser, or as a last resort, to another child's room.

But you are not forced to clean, so you get no reduced fire risk, no reduced lost-child risk, and no finding of treasures you thought were lost or stolen as you unearth places in your room that have not seen daylight in years, possibly since you moved in. All of these are blessings, and to avoid the cliché, these blessings are not in disguise.

If you simply do not have room in your master bedroom for shelves, don't default to a kid's room. I suggest you do what millions of Americans are doing, often without knowing it: Store your year's supply of food and clothing inside your couch.

The main advantage of this storage technique is it can both dry and store the food simultaneously. Many people think commercial dehydrators and freeze dryers are the best methods to dry food for storage. And our dehydrator will dry edible food—when my wife runs it. But for me, the couch can dry food faster, with less hassle and no expended electricity.

I simply feed the kids some pizza, spaghetti, even toast on the couch. In two days, I simply lift the cushions to find whole slices of pizza, entire spaghetti servings, and various slices of toast completely dried and preserved. (At our house, a qualified "whole" slice of pizza or toast is one with less than three bites missing. Spaghetti is harder to tell if bites are gone, but if you can tell, it is *not* a full serving to us. Your household definitions may vary.)

Many pizza brands are just as tasty dehydrated as fresh, particularly if I had to cook or heat the pizza in the oven. And the flavor remains intact over long periods, sometimes for days.

Now I am not suggesting that a slice of couch-preserved pizza that I cooked would taste as good as manna in the wilderness, unless you mean the manna you picked up on Sunday that was full of worms and rot. The pizza I cook *is* tasty enough that worms and rot race for it. But my pizza isn't as good as the manna you could pick up on Monday through Saturday.

And speaking of ancient dried foods, one of the most famous food dehydrators and storers of the past was King Herod. He strengthened a fort at Masada, a mount by the Dead Sea. The King planned on hiding there if he ever lost power and could not get out of the country to safety. He stored a supply of food large enough to last many years there.

During excavation, someone found some dehydrated beans in a room that held Herod's several-year supply. The beans were reportedly still recognizable as beans and still nutritious to eat, even though they were 2,000 years old. But no one has found any evidence of a commercial dehydrator, which leads me to believe Herod dried all of his food in his couch. So this technique *likely* has ancient precedence.

Having raised six boys, and thus having decades of experience drying various foods and other sundries in couches, I am convinced that most pizzas could be stored in a couch for dozens, if not hundreds, of years and not lose any flavors or nutritional value. Most pizza slices would still be recognizable decades later. Couches do not make pizza shrivel, wrinkle, or turn black like a normal dehydrator. Slices are preserved in living color.

Another useful feature of a couch dehydrator compared to a commercial one is the couch hides food odor. When my wife dries jerky in the dehydrator, the aroma fills the house, and the family's mouths water all day. (When I dry food, their noses and eyes water all day.)

But when something is dehydrated in the couch, even something I cooked, we can't smell the food over the normal smells in the house. The kids leave it alone. So far, neighbors have never bothered it. Even the dog won't touch it. It's safe.

Once the pizza is dry in the couch, leave it under the cushions. Removing it exposes it to air-borne bacteria, moisture, and still-hungry children. If the slices remain in place under the cushions, they will work their way into the corner pockets of the couch.

Once the food is in those pockets, it historically has been safe from thieves, worms, ants, varmints, earthquakes, and even fire. No one cleans those corner pockets, so what could be a safer, more secure, long-term storage place?

However, a word of warning may be useful here about storing bottled or canned food in a hide-a-bed couch. The metal hinges that allow the mattress and bed frame to rise out of and sink back into the couch frame can crack or shatter glass jars and pinch or tear metal cans, which in many cases can render the food inedible.

Bags of flour, sugar, wheat, and rice can easily puncture or rip on those hinges. A hole in a bag allows commodities to drip or even cascade to the floor, possibly even out of the corner pockets of the couch. Once on the floor, the contents are exposed to ants, mice, children, pets, and even neighbors. Thus no longer preserved in safety, those contents will be lost for future use.

If you avoid these pitfalls and have enough food for several months securely stored in your couch, you can turn your attention to storing clothing. The easiest way to keep clothing in your couch is to fold laundry on it for several weeks. In that time, enough socks, shirts, pants, dresses, and even the occasional winter coat will find their way into the couch so that, when you need to, you can clothe your family for a year.

A top advantage favoring this approach is you don't miss the clothes stored this way. You don't notice they are gone for several weeks. Then you watch for them for more weeks, but they don't show up, so you assume the dryer ate them, and you give up on finding them. Clothes in, under, and behind the couch seem to be stored safer than if they were placed in an all-cedar closet piled high with mothballs.

Every sock or other article of clothing that I have dug out from in or around the couch has been pristinely preserved, once I got the dust and hair cleaned off so I could see the preservation. This process reminds me of the Sphinx in Egypt, preserved under all that sand for centuries.

Another advantage of the couch over an entire room for food and clothing storage is the couch holds so much more per square inch than a room. My wife and I have measured the amount of material taken from the couch when we do spring cleaning, which in our home occurs in September because we are so far behind, but I am sure you can get the same results in March or April.

We have removed five laundry baskets of clothes from the couch in one cleaning. And that wasn't including the food, which was another eight boxes full. We could have stored a lot more food and clothes if it weren't for the 12 boxes of toys being aged in there as well.

Once the boxes and baskets were full, we piled them next to the couch sections, and these full containers actually occupied more space than the couch did on its own. The couch showed no signs of collapse or shrinkage with the items removed, and it wasn't noticeably more comfortable. These boxes and baskets took up a lot of space in the empty room, yet they seemed to take no space in the couch.

I do not understand how this physics law works, how a couch can seem to take no more space than normal, and can hold boxes and baskets of extra toys, clothing, and foodstuffs. You may be a clean freak that does not believe your couch can or should contain *any* additional items; I wouldn't have accepted it either if I had not accomplished it. You can try it as an experiment for the sake of science if nothing else.

The ocean seems to work on this same principle. Surely you have read in the news about the Great Pacific Garbage Patch (GPGP for short), the floating garbage pile in the ocean that is twice the size of the state of Texas. You would think that so much garbage would cause the oceans to rise at least a foot or two since there are many of these garbage piles out there. But so far, the sea appears to be using the law of couch physics to absorb it.

Some of you may object to storing food and clothing in the same place. You can solve this dilemma by simply storing your clothes behind and under your washer and dryer and only storing food in your couch. With this strategy, you can more easily remove your clothes from dusty storage and wash them when you need them.

I strongly recommend, however, that you don't store the food by the washer and dryer, no matter how strong the temptation to do so grips you. We have tried drying food in a clothes dryer, but the constant rolling is enough to break down any food into tiny crumbs, even the cookies I bake. And though my cookies are certainly easier to eat this way, and they are somewhat easier to keep down, it is impossible to get all of the crumbs out of the dryer, so your clothes will come out speckled with crumbs for weeks.

Another seeming advantage to storing food near the clothes washer is the ease of rehydrating dried food. I recommend that you use a dish instead. Washers are prone to have a soap film inside, and though such a taste improves the flavor of anything I cook, it does not help what my wife cooks, often rendering her food inedible, even for our six boys—hearty eaters, all.

Once you have settled on storing food and clothes in your couch, or food in the couch with clothes under and behind your washer and dryer, you may be tempted, because of the superior security and less expense, to store your valuable documents in your couch also. Items like journals and diaries, family group sheets and written histories, photo albums, wills, deeds, and paper money should *not* be stored in the corner pockets of a couch unless the paper is laminated. (Coins also can be stored in a couch with no adverse or long-term effects.)

Usually, laminating paper money renders it illegal tender. And jam, honey, milk in baby bottles, and a diaper or two always find their way into the couch pockets. Such items often make using documents difficult, if not impossible, unless you intend to preserve the paperwork purposely to eat with the other food. Then storing documents in jam or honey is a good idea.

Some of you may still want to store your year's supply the customary way, by turning a room of your house into a food and clothing store. And you may want to store your valuable documents and heirlooms in a safe or locking file cabinet. And a few good reasons exist for storing and preserving items this way.

But if you have no spare room, or if you want to use the room for something else, the couch alternative is undoubtedly viable for many people. And if you are like us, storing food and clothing this way, you will not need to adjust the way you currently live.

# A Twisted Tale

## *Richard Crawford*

More than a half-century ago, being a young man embarking on a career as a repairman of electronic devices designed for entertainment, TV, radio, stereo, car radio, etc. I started my career in Weber County and soon discovered that the three commercial stations would broadcast new programs for nine months, then mostly reruns in June, July, and August. Many people decided that watching reruns were not worth the cost of a repair, so they left the set alone till September. Being obsessed with keeping busy all year, I found that St. George was the place to spend summers since people would sit in front of their swamp coolers watching TV. Employment was easy to obtain in 1964 and 1965 when St. George had 5,500 people.

One day I went to a gentleman's home to repair his TV. As I was working on the TV, he asked if I was related to an individual he had grown up with. I replied that the person he mentioned was my dad. Then he told me a story about my father that surprised me. It turns out that he was my dad's cousin, and both of them were born and raised in Springdale. He said that every Tuesday night during the summers, Young men and Young Women gathered on the tennis court behind the elementary school for a dance.

He said that my dad would occasionally encourage some pretty young lady to accompany him to his car. He drove a 1927 Chevy Coupe. The gentleman whose name was Gerald said that one night he decided to see where they went, so after they got in the car, Gerald jumped on the rear bumper and rode along, hanging on tight. The rear window of the car was tiny, so the driver could not see his stowaway.

Dad drove into the Mount Carmel tunnel in Zion National Park and parked in one of the many Windows that afforded a view of the canyon below. Then as he stopped the car, Gerald jumped off the bumper and slid underneath the vehicle out of sight. As the couple enjoyed the beautiful view, Dad would tell the girl about previous cave-ins in the tunnel. Then the girl would get scared and jump into his arms for comfort. When the couple got back in the car and started it up, Gerald crawled out from under and jumped back on the bumper for the ride back to Springdale.

After I finished repairing his TV, Gerald observed that I needed a haircut. He stated that he had often cut my dad's hair in their youth and wanted to relive memories by cutting my hair. He did a good job and wouldn't accept any payment for it. That night I returned to my uncle's home where I was staying for the summer. I told him what had happened. He commented that I was probably the only TV repairman that would go on a house call and come back with a free haircut. Then he shared some additional memories of my mom and dad's early marriage.

Later, I returned north for the winter. (Yes, I know, ordinary people go south for the winter; I kind of live my life backward.) I told Mom and dad the story of my encounter with Gerald. Dad was surprised and said that he had no idea that Gerald had done that, but it was the kind of thing Gerald would do, and it explained some mysteries from that time. Dad had a sneaky grin on his face. Mom looked surprised, then broke into a huge smile as she said, "That's how he got ME."

# Always Relying on the Kindness of Strangers

*Eric R Jensen*

Many of you are parents and can probably relate to children going through phases or chapters of their young lives when they emulate their favorite superheroes, sports, or otherwise. Well, our son's favorite hero besides myself, of course, was Spiderman. Every single day during that summer, Austinn wore his Spiderman suit from sun up to sundown. He wore it to the swimming pool, to the playground, to his summer school acting camp, also while regular camping, he even wore it to church, albeit underneath his white shirt. We couldn't get him to take it off. We tried everything we could think of to get him to wear shorts or a different shirt or even a different superhero costume... All to no avail. He *loved* Spiderman.

So, we just resigned ourselves to the fact that our boy would be Spiderman until he didn't want to be anymore. Well, one day, the strangest thing happened. He put on a Batman costume. I don't know why or how, but there he was... completely Batman clad from head to toe. I can't say I was happy to see it, because it was an even hotter month of the summer now, and as we know, black attracts sunlight. I asked him to please change back into his Spiderman costume. At least it was lighter and made for easier air-flow around his sweaty, stinky, little body, But for whatever reason, my words fell upon deaf ears. He was Batman for the day.

As part of my OBT (Off Broadway Theater) duties, I always have to go to Sam's Club to pick up concession items and then haul them into our theater before the show each night. My son, of course, always helped me as a good little boy does. After we loaded up the truck, we parked in the alley behind the theater, right in the heart of downtown Salt Lake, and carted the goods into the lobby. Austinn got in the back of the truck and started handing me the cans of soda pop, snickers bars, bags of popcorn, and whatever other concessions we needed for the night.

Suddenly, an unknown handsome stranger walked by. He looked into the back of our truck and smiled at the cuteness of the little Batboy helping his father. The man exclaimed confidently, "Excuse me there, Batman…" He had my son's attention. "Thank you for helping out our poor old age citizens and keeping our city safe. On behalf of all the Salt Lakers… we thank you!"

Austinn smiled and saluted the man heartily, then said, "You're welcome, citizen. Please stay safe!" The man practically fell on the ground laughing but was able to walk away, assuring us that he would.

I saw nothing but twinkling eyes and a grin from ear to ear underneath that Batman Cowell. Austinn, then helped me get the rest of the concession items into the theater, and as we were unloading them at the snack bar, he said to me… "Dad, I'm Batman from now on."

# 'Twas the Day After Christmas

## *Don Miles*

'Twas the day after Christmas
    And all through the house
The kids were all running
    Over Mom's new white blouse.
The stockings were strewn
    Everywhere without care.
The candy that filled them
    Was stuck to my chair.

The boys were at war
    With all their new stuff.
The weight machine pounded;
    My wife was getting buff.
I spoke not a word
    As I rose from my bed
For the TV was blaring
    *Snow White and Rose Red.*

Then from the kitchen
    Came the sound of a platter
Hitting the floor
    As if it would splatter.
I ran in to see
    What damage was done.
The children all saw me
    And started to run.

# Utah's Special Blend

Barricades of cookie crumbs
    Covered the floor,
Shielding army men and tanks
    From the destruction of war.
I called to the boys,
    And meekly they came.
"This kitchen floor," I exclaimed,
    "Will ne'er be the same."

"These cookie crumb barricades,
    You can see in a flash,
Aren't professionally done.
    They are easy to smash."
So we got out the Legos,
    Lincoln Logs, and Construx,
Waffle Blocks, wood blocks,
    And yellow dump trucks.

We proceeded to build,
    To make, to expand.
Compared to this stuff
    Watching movies seemed bland.
We played all that day,
    And left the toys out all night.
The next morning we continued
    To the children's delight.

Before we knew it
    The weekend was spent.
The battles were over,
    The barricades all rent.
The next Monday morning
    As I rode back to work
I wondered how in the world
    I had gone so berserk.

My memory was flashing
    The boys' laughter and smiles
As we played out their wars
    Full of strategies and wiles.
So right there I vowed
    With all of my might,
"I'll play with my kids
    After work ev'ry night."

# Creature

## *Tim Keller*

*Creature from Black Lake* (1975) ranks to this day among the scariest movies I've ever seen. Perhaps it has something to do with the way and where I grew up. The Wasatch Mountain range in northern Utah boasts all manner of remote wilderness, lakes, and rivers and tall tales of the creatures within. Creatures like the Sasquatch, Manitou, even the Bear Lake Monster factored heavily in the campfire tales of my youth.

Having recently acquired Netflix, I undertook the viewing of some formative favorites through the lens of adulthood. I placed my request and was informed that while obscure, the title existed in another region. It would take some time to arrive. I worried as I waited. Would it measure up? Or would it, like so many other childhood obsessions, turn out to be an incredible cheese-fest?

When at last the telltale Netflix-red envelope arrived, it was all I could do to get through the workday. On my way home, I bought some suitably trashy movie snacks, turned off the lights, and began.

The film is campy, no doubt. The setting is a slice of small-town Americana; the characters are mostly likable country folk, kind of a monster meets Mayberry sort of thing. It was easy to chuckle at my childhood-self—at first. But the film also plays expertly on our fears at a primal level. The creature's roar— the darkness, even the daylight scenes take place in closed cover – and we don't get a clear view of the creature until the last scenes in the film. Even my father (mom wisely refused to see it), a formidable man and war veteran besides had jumped several times.

The film opens with a couple of *Deliverance* looking woodsmen rowing their canoe into the backcountry to do some hunting. Unlike *Deliverance*, however, the men are friendly, kind, and the depth of their bromance was obvious.

The boat slams to a halt. Thinking they're hung up on something, the bow-man reaches under the boat to free them. That's when a giant hairy arm explodes from the surface, flings him out of the boat and under the water, where after an intense, albeit useless struggle, the man disappears. Only pieces of him are ever found. Traumatic stuff for a nine-year-old.

That scene, however, is nothing compared to the one in which the unfortunate trapper's compatriot relates his tale to the police.

"Eight feet tall," he says. "300 pounds!" he says.

... I remember 300 pounds— I passed that particular milestone sometime last year. Apparently, by 1975 standards at least, I now over-match my childhood's greatest fear.

It wasn't always like this. On the day of my high school graduation, I stood 6ft tall and weighed in at a svelte 152 pounds. But hey, I'm a victim of evolution, or rather, the glacial pace thereof. Ancestors on my father's side were Vikings, who, according to at least one Discovery channel documentary, pillaged my mother's Anglo-Saxon ancestors for generations. The results of which are obvious. My body clearly evolved for maximum mayhem; to battle bears and pillage villages, all on a Snickers-sized piece of whale blubber.

That's strike one. Strike two is being raised Mormon. Don't get me wrong, Mormons are perfectly nice people, but food is a huge part of Mormon culture. Even the once a month fast lasts only a single meal and generally serves only to whet the appetite in preparation for an afternoon of unbridled gluttony. Based on those factors alone, one can conclude that slender adulthood was never going to happen.

Alas, I also love food. Hostess Ding Dongs in particular—and pizza and Big Mac's and Burritos and everything in between— and not just the food. I love the experience of food, from fine dining to road-trip-food-mart-forays, to settling down for an evening of late-night television—a heavy-laden tray of forbidden fruit (or fruit loops) before me.

Sunday dinner funeral potatoes, and Roast whatever, and why not?—Life is too short for subsisting on tofu and weed salad only. Besides, I've been known to rationalize—I'm not fat, just heavily built, big-boned, husky even. And heck, I can always go on a diet.

Still, every so often, these warning signs pop up—little things, like outweighing Bigfoot. — Or the time three heroically proportioned friends and I lifted the table off the floor by squeezing into a restaurant booth. Or the time the Desperado Roller Coaster's 4 G's of acceleration blew every seam out of my Levis. That was so humiliating. What choice did I have but to ride it five more times?

Amusement parks can be excellent barometers of one's "personal growth." Take, for instance, a trip to Lagoon amusement park in Farmington, Utah, so epic in its scope that my friend wrote about it in his column.

Alex, and Shelby, who each run around 130 pounds soaking wet. Plus Courtney, and myself, who can best be described as "full-figured," were in line for the Wild Mouse. When at last we reached the front of the line, Alex jumped in with Shelby, leaving the rear seat for us.

At which time, the somewhat flummoxed ride attendant asked: "Would you gentlemen prefer separate cars?"

To be honest, we thought the question odd, rude even. I mean, why should we want to ride separately? A quick glance confirmed that Shelby and Alex were already strapped in, so we ignored the attendant's query and jumped into the car. At which point Courtney's left butt cheek and my right came to a painful halt about halfway in, leaving several inches of open space between our Gluteus-Maximi and the seat. A situation made worse by the ride attendant's performance of the Heimlich maneuver with the restraint bar.

We couldn't even fasten the seat belt around us both, and the car had already begun to move before we concluded this might be a horrible, terrible, no good, very bad idea. In desperation, we each wrapped an end around our wrists. "Grab me if I start to fly out," he joked. "We shall never speak of this!" I responded, and other than my relation of this tale here, and his column; we have not.

As our car began its agonizingly slow climb to the top, we became almost preternaturally aware of the creaks and groans of metal being stressed to its near breaking point. Our faces pointed heavenward during the ascent, and all I could think about was showing up at the pearly gates whereupon we would be forced to admit to being ejected from the Wild Mouse on the third turn from the top, plummeting 100 feet to the ground, and crushing a churro kiosk.

In descent, the car became a speeding blubbernaught of death, careening along the track at supernatural velocity. We shrieked until only bats and dogs could hear us.

Fortunately, we were wedged so tight that no real movement was possible. We lived to tell the tale, swearing never to ride together again.

A pact I must admit to having broken on more than one occasion.

Actually, I've kind of gotten used to things like being a mobile amusement park attraction. One day while relaxing at a local pool, a diminutive shadow fell upon me. "Mister," a lad of undetermined age asked. "Umm, are you going down the slide again?"

Slowly I turned, fixing this upstart with the chilliest of gazes. "I might. Why?"

Apparently, his interest had to do with physics, what with water displacement being what it is. And so, they followed me, he and his friends, pied piper style, to line up along the landing pool where they celebrated my splash down at the base of water slides yelling, "Blllllasst off!"

While life's little reminders, taken, on the whole, prove beyond doubt that I am, in fact, not just heavy, not husky, and not merely big-boned. (I'm fairly certain if you can grab a handful of bone and jiggle it, you should probably see a doctor.) Oh, I've been those things … and skinny and built as well.

Pride forces me at this point to halt this essay of self-deprecation long enough to explain that I am, in fact, active, more so than most. I do ranch work, yard work, and walk every night. I also hunt, fish, hike, swim, and on occasion, take the stairs. And I've tried the diets, but even the advice of the much-vaunted Dr. Atkins failed in the face of Mother Nature. A steak without potatoes, after all, is really just a slab of dead cow.

Growing older (not to mention larger) is not for sissies, but like so many things, I've made my peace with the passage of time.

Would I rather be thin again? Of course. And maybe someday, my plane will crash in the Andes, and it will happen. I can see it now, after months of unparalleled suffering, of watching my fitter traveling companions succumb, until at long last, too demoralized to go on, I strip to my tattered skivvies, stretch forth my limbs, and leap from a precipice only to discover my ability to glide, squirrel-like to the safety of the valley below.

Barring that, just thinking about it is exhausting. Would someone please pass the Ding Dongs?

# Tiny Little Towel

## *James D Beers*

My son Joseph has always been prone to listen with rapt attention, and bug-eyed amazement to every story whistled over the dentured-gums of old-timers. Occasionally, he'll even listen to *me* (a non-old-timer…at least for the moment) carry on about some bygone occurrence. But only when he's a captive audience, like when I have him cornered in the car on a long drive or trapped in a tent during a camping trip. Most of the time, he's incredulous of my adventured past. I'm not sure why—repetition, maybe? Perhaps my propensity for exaggeration? Lack of witnesses? Cryptozoological references? Whatever the reason, our story sessions don't often turn out well, like during a recent trip home from one of Joe's Little League games.

"Dad, there's no way you counted *coup* on a moose." The emphasis on "coup" rang heavy, especially between Joe's air quotes.

"Did too," I swore with the Scout Sign. "Snuck up on him, slapped his dewlap, and got away before he could stomp me."

"Yeah," Joe laid on the sarcasm, spreading it thick like peanut butter. "Just like the time you *outran* Bigfoot or when you managed to stave off a horde of bald-faced hornets with a *weedeater*."

"Oh, that's a good one!" I waved my finger and settled in for a long-winder. "Happened in '95, two years after I outran the Big Fellow. You wouldn't believe how those hornets came pourin' out of the ground, all foamin' at the mouth and totin' daggers—"

Apparently, Joe's ears waxed over, and all he heard between there and the house was a bunch of "Blah, blah, yada, yada, yada…"

Fortunately, I haven't ruined the kid's appetite for stories from *other* sources...just from yours truly.

Certainly, Joe gets his fill of tall tales, yarns, legends, adventures and the like in the school classroom, from the pulpit at church, and probably here and there from his own version of the school-ground "under the jungle-gym congregation." The annual family reunions themselves are virtual smorgasbords of yarn-spinning. However, most humdingers that he remembers and retells are picked up while tagging along on my home visits to older folks from our Mormon Church wards in Utah. If you get him going, you're bound to hear a tale or two from Brother Phillips or Sister Witlock.

Of all the yarns and stories, though, the one that he recounts the most comes from a ninety-six-year-old World War II veteran we visited during Christmas a couple of years ago.

***

"We didn't have any indoor plumbing except a hand-cranked pump at Mother's kitchen sink." From the recliner in his own private room of the George E. Whalen Veteran's Home in Ogden, Utah, Fred Wilson reached back in time through almost 100 years of memories. A blue baseball cap embroidered with the word "veteran" in capital letters and festooned with pins sat high on his head. His eyes twinkled beneath bushy white eyebrows and through wire-rimmed glasses.

"Really?" Joe sounded both amazed and incredulous.

"That's right! And Dad didn't have the money to put any in until after I left home in '41. Joined the Navy at seventeen and sent home most of my pay."

Fred and I saw the wheels turning in Joseph's head as his eyebrows wriggled into a scrunch.

"I know what you're thinking," Fred laughed through a wry smile. "We had two outhouses, and each week Mother gave all eight of us a bath in the washtub."

"All *eight* of you at the same time?!"

"Oh, no!" Fred leaned forward in his chair, still smiling. "She'd line us up naked in the barn, and one-by-one, we'd stand in the metal tub filled with suds until she scrubbed us down with a brush and rinsed us off with a pitcher of water."

Fred obviously enjoyed telling this story, especially to a young boggled audience like Joseph. And somehow, it sounded familiar to me like I'd heard it before, but I couldn't quite put my finger on it.

"Then we'd squeal on back to the house wrapped in a towel, a blanket, or sometimes a gunnysack." The old soldier let out a laugh buried somewhere deep in his lungs, slapped the armrest, and settled back in his chair. "Made for a mighty cold run in the winter!"

***

On the drive home, I chuckled over Fred's story. "What'd you think of that one, Joe?"

Joseph snickered a couple of times too. "Eight naked kids in a row, waiting for a bath—that'd be terrible standing there nude with your brothers and sisters! Even more embarrassing than when *you* got your head stuck in the chair during Sunday school!"

"Oh, I don't know about that," I smiled, surprised he brought up one of my own childhood's not-so-shining moments—apparently, he'd listened to at least one of my yarns.

"Ah, come on! How many times have you had to stand in line naked with your brother and sisters waiting for a bath?"

"Well—" I was about to tell him that my childhood home was built plumbed and that his grandma stopped bathing us kids together when I was about five, but that's when I realized why Fred's story sounded so familiar. There had been a washtub...of sorts. And there had been a line of us naked kids waiting for a bath—just not solely a sibling affair.

"Actually," I restarted, "there was an instance of similar...uh...communal bathing, as I recall."

Joe shifted in his seat and gave me the same astonished and incredulous look he gave Fred.

I don't know what Fred's age was when—or if—he ever escaped the naked bath line (perhaps it *was* when he left home at seventeen), but at the time *I* stood naked in line for a bath, I felt certain I was *way* too old to be wandering about in my birthday suit.

"I think it was in the summer of 1987—" I began.

Joe was still listening.

**\*\*\***

"—and every summer before then and every summer until I left home, we spent several days cleaning up Grandma Gaver's house and property in Salmon, Idaho. Uncles, aunts, cousins, and sometimes friends would gather to drag junk out of Grandma's house, various sheds, a barn, an unoccupied pigeon coop, an old school bus, and a couple of farm fields."

My parents always called it the family vacation, but us kids knew better; it meant several days of child slavery. Our only recourse was the wild and raucous cousin campouts in Grandma's yard, and the never-ending flow of candy and Hostess treats lovingly gifted right from Grandma's generous hands.

Crazy stuff happened during those summer trips—one of my cousins ran over his brother's leg with a truck (it was an accident), kids played with fire, and important stuff got burned (to adults everything is important). Uncle Lem showed us how to conduct a cow pregnancy test (trust me, you don't want to know), and I once caught gastrointestinal enteritis (trust me, you don't want to know). But the worst of the worst was when Aunt Trudy and Aunt Ethel forced public bathings.

"...For years, one of the principal projects my dad and uncles worked on was the mystery surrounding the property's water supply. To put it bluntly, Grandma's water smelled like the aftermath of a chili cook-off and produced similar results if you were brave enough to drink it. During one stay, the water stunk so bad that people were afraid to turn on any faucets. For Aunt Trudy and Aunt Ethel, this was a major blow. Regular showers and baths were their religion. I later thought that it was no wonder all of their combined fifteen kids are so skinny—they scrubbed off half of their skin during the developing years."

115

"…After a few days of stinky kids running around Grandma's house, Aunt Trudy and Aunt Ethel had had enough. They drove downtown to Kings, bought a kiddie pool and a giant bottle of Clorox, and came back and set up shop on Grandma's front lawn. We unsuspecting kids were finishing up a lunch of peanut butter and jelly sandwiches at Grandma's kitchen bar when Aunt Ethel burst through the front door wearing an apron, rubber gloves, and shop glasses."

"All right, all you stinky kids, line up!" she barked, pointing to a spot on the carpet in front of her.

We stared at her gape-mouthed, wondering what stinky kids she was talking about.

"That means all y'all!" Aunt Ethel lived in Georgia for some time and had picked up some Southern words and a slight accent, which really came alive when she got excited. She was generally mild-manner and quite nice, but right then, she could've been a commanding officer in the Civil War's Confederate Army.

Several of the teenagers skedaddled, escaping out the back door. I was one of the unlucky dozen hypnotized by Aunt Ethel's fear-inducing gaze. The lot of us lined up in front of her bug-eyed, and shaking in our fake leather cowboy boots and cutoff jean shorts.

"All y'all take off your clothes 'cause you're goin' outside to take a bath."

None of us moved, unsure if this were some kind of weird practical joke. In my own mind, I wondered what could possibly be wrong with Grandma's bathroom bathtub. Before I could ask, and at about the same time, I remembered the stinky water situation; Aunt Ethel barked out another command.

"LET'S GO!"

We—boy and girl cousins alike!—started stripping as if our clothes were on fire. I was reasonably sure that public nudity was a federal offense but was so scared at the time that I couldn't voice a warning.

"Okay, now, march!" Aunt Ethel ordered, gesturing for us to depart through the front door.

Every naked one of us piled outside without question.

On the front lawn, Aunt Trudy was filling the kiddie pool with a hose and stirring in the Clorox with the handle end of a garden hoe.

"Okay, six of you at a time," she said, dropping the hoe and grabbing a bottle of dish soap. The youngest six of our group crowded into the pool, and Aunt Trudy and Aunt Ethel went to scrubbing.

I've since seen sheep dippings done with hooked poles that were more humane."

When the first six were done, the remaining five cousins and I clambered into the pool, each one of us still bearing the same bug-eyed looks of terror with which we started the fiasco. Like Aunt Ethel, Aunt Trudy wore an apron, rubber gloves, and shop glasses. The two of them could've been mad scientists in an old horror flick the way they looked and carried on with their humiliating experiment.

I didn't have the sense nor the time to protest the bath, partly because the fear hadn't yet worn off, but mostly because Aunt Trudy had grabbed me by the arms, dunked me a couple times, and then scrubbed parts of me that I didn't know needed cleaning.

When it was over, we were rushed back inside Grandma's house and handed towels. I should say, rather, that *some* of us were handed towels. I was given a washcloth, a little square of terry cloth no bigger than a potholder. By then, the fear was beginning to wear off, and humiliation was sinking heavily upon me. Try as I might, I couldn't get the tiny little towel to cover both of my hush-hush areas simultaneously. I was hoping it would go unnoticed, but it's not every day you see a naked eleven-year-old boy trying to both dry off and hide himself with a towel half the size of his underwear.

And that's when Aunt Ethel sealed the embarrassment.

"Why Jimmy," she said with a touch of Southern accent, "I can see both your privates!"

I instantly dropped the washcloth and hurriedly put my clothes on, grumbling under my breath and cursing my shared heritage with those two crazy ladies.

"That's probably why—" I was going to tell Joe that a possible reason for my poor sleep and general fidgety behavior at the annual family reunion may subconsciously be on account of events like the 1987 forced public bathing, but he was too busy laughing.

117

\*\*\*

Ever since Fred regaled us with his washtub tale, Joe will bring it up whenever he needs a good laugh. I like to think it's because I always follow up Fred's story with the tiny little towel incident. Whatever the case, it appears the story is better than the usual "blah, blah, yada, yada, yada."

Either that or I might be getting a little long in the tooth.

brotherly riff-raff in the horse trough, it was great fun if you had the companionship of a duck or two in there with you. And if you found a few tadpoles, it was like finding gold. Granted, you'd have to check for snakes before you jump in. Those white underwear pants would never be white again. No amount of bleach that Mother used would ever brighten them up, but that's no worry for a kid. I'm surprised we never got an eye infection or skin rash from the horse slobber, germs, and green mossy slime in that water. Likewise, there's no accurate estimation of how much water we swallowed as we dunked each other. We never thought about it. Good memories from a family farm when I was a kid.

Perhaps you favor the old slip-and-slide on the neighbor's yard. Mom might have warned you that it was dangerous and not to go over there, but what's summer without a yard attraction like that? Maneuvers performed on the neighborhood slip-and-slide could surpass anything you might see today on the Olympic balance beam, parallel bars, or rings. And let's just say, if a kid broke their arm, well, you had a big story to tell when you went back to school in the fall. I was scared of the slip-and-slide, but Lloyd was quite a daredevil on that contraption. I suspect that's where he acquired his first surfing skills by being able to stay up on his feet no matter what object was thrown at him. I felt it was best to watch from the sidelines and cool down with a peripheral splash or two that might hit me. The slip-and-slide was not for me.

Water balloon battles were the personal quest of many kids. It remains a mystery to me where the secret hiding place was for all those water-filled balloons. They seemed to come out when you least expected it. During sweltering summer, it was nice to experience a wet cool down once in a while. But when a kid starts to develop welts because they're the target too many times, or their eyeglasses get busted, the fun begins to run out. Using a slingshot to launch the water balloons was very popular. Most summers, we never dried out. Take the trash out…splat, from somewhere over the fence. Sweep the side patio…splat, from some unknown direction. Go to the shed to retrieve something for Mom…splat, right in the back, and no one in sight. Sometimes, you would hate to turn the lights off at night to go to sleep for fear that "someone" would creep up during the night and...splat. Despite being a victim while sleeping, your parents would likely blame you for the watery mess. Of course, there was no confession by the mysterious instigator.

Who could forget riding tricycles, bicycles, or roller skates down the sidewalk as your parents or the neighbors watered their lawn with a hand-held garden hose? If you dared them, they would spray you pretty good. Many kids could be heard squealing for hours at a time as they rode up and down the sidewalk, probably a hundred times or more, getting sprayed over and over. All the while, the yard got a good drink of water too. There was no shortage of happy faces and smiles by kids and adults during that water recreation event.

Water guns, water pistols, and a bucket full of soaked sponges were on the wish list of many kids, and they would beg for them. The more, the better was the silent rule, and it was surprising that no kid got a hernia from lifting their substantial arsenal of water-filled weaponry. Those were the days before backpacks, and you had to be creative to tote a sizeable load of water-filled ammunition. That was when the little red wagon came in handy for many kids. Sometimes there was no time to refill or reload; reach for another water-filled balloon or water gun ready for use. It was the stuff that made for hours of good fun, even if some kids insisted that they needed to wear an army helmet, diving mask, or snorkel for the battle.

Sometimes the backyard kiddie pool was used for its intended purpose, but it was more often used as the neutral zone for quick dunk and refill of water guns. It was every boy or girl for themselves. It was serious. No one wants a teammate whose aim isn't good enough to avoid a nearby hornet's nest. And forget about trusting the family dog. No doggie treat of any kind can win a dog's allegiance to remain quiet when you're strategically hiding for the perfect moment of attack. There would be a few unforgettable lessons learned, such as the fact that one should never walk underneath the support branches that hold up a tree fort. Buckets of water crashing onto your head would be a reminder for years. It didn't matter if you were taking out the trash for Mom, on your way to retrieve a tool from the tool shed for Dad, or taking your bike out of the yard for a bike ride. You would have a hard time staying upright on your feet when that watery force came down on your head. It would be a never-forgotten experience, and revenge would certainly be planned.

The neighborhood creek with the swinging rope offered many artful launches and drops. It was inspiring to see the summersaults, twists, turns, and in-air freeze poses. Unbelievable heights could be reached if you jumped up high in the air with the rope before swinging out over the creek. Tremendous cannonball splashes could be made from such a drop, potentially causing a tsunami. Unavoidably, a swimsuit or two would spontaneously be lost on impact in the water. But such an occurrence is good storytelling material in years to follow. We never checked the water for parasites, amoebas, or anything else that could make us sick. The thought never occurred to us. It's a testament that none of us ever became sick from that murky creek water. Thank goodness we never saw any water snakes. But if we ever would have found any snakes, I'm sure Lloyd would've captured them and launched them into the woods, far away from our water hole. Come to think of it; that's probably why any ducks ran for their life when they saw us on-foot heading to the creek.

Good memories from my youth and plenty of smiles were stirred simply by taking our grandkids to Peach City Drive-in on that summer evening. I hope such diners and drive-ins never go out of fashion. They're a treasured part of Utah living, families, and good memories. The next time you pass by one of those fancy modern water recreation attractions, remind yourself of the origin of the *real* water amusement parks of the earlier generations. Spare yourself the high admission price of the high-rise twisted steel, fiberglass tubes, and cement pools at today's water theme parks. Simply reach for your garden hose. Make some priceless memories at the *real* water amusement park—home style. And if you don't have a nostalgic eatery like Brigham City's Peach City Drive-In, the old hand-crank ice cream maker still yields great tasting rewards! Happy summer, and stay cool out there!

# Fry Sauce

## *Jon Baty*

Fry sauce has been a staple to any Utah meal. Mashed potatoes get its gravy, mac gets its cheese, Jell-o gets its fruit and is called salad (?), and everything else is doused in fry sauce. And while many Utahns have their own recipes and fry sauce needs, the story of how fry sauce came to be has rarely been told. The media and your alt-right Uncle will claim that this heralded delicacy was developed in a local fast-food chain; however the real story has never been truthfully recorded: UNTIL NOW.

Dr. Seever Beamons, a tenured professor at Shiphole Community College, has extensively investigated the tasty phenomenon that has taken over Utah, Southern Idaho, and parts of Thpain. Through his research, Dr. Beamons stumbled upon the roots of fry sauce.

"The earliest inhabitants of the area now known as Utah were called Paleo-Indians, who later developed into the Fremont and Anasazi people, roughly around 500 AD," Dr. Beamons says. "These ancient Native Americans 'painted' the Canyonlands of Utah. The painting style is known as the Barrier Canyon Style, named after Utah's Barrier Canyon, which I understand was named after Ted 'Sweet Tea' Barrier, the first white man to yell his name in the canyon, to hear his name echo."

When pressed on this newly discovered knowledge, Dr. Beamons reiterates, "Records of this yelling have been passed down through Native American tales, wherein Ted's name roughly translates to 'Foolish Man Who Won't Stop Yelling as We Try to Sleep.'"

As many know, throughout Barrier Canyon's "Great Gallery," you find numerous paintings depicting a warrior holding a small stick-like object. Dr. Beamons believes that these drawings represent someone holding an Anasazi delicacy: a cut-up potato, which seems to have been fried. "This is the first true recorded instance of the French fry," Dr. Beamons states. Although most historians and scientists have outright and fully disputed this "historical fact," Dr. Beamons insists that there is no other way to explain the drawing he briefly saw in a picture, displayed in a pamphlet, found in a Moab area tourist store.

"I know what I saw," Dr. Beamons notes. "And I have devoted the last eight months of my life to explain this unrecorded truth in Utah history. Also, the earth is flat, and immunizations are ways for the government to control the people."

Essa Shiphole, the founder of Shiphole Community College, fully backs the professor's findings. "We put our trust in Dr. Beamons," Ms. Shiphole says. "Plus, we pay him at least $28,000 a year, so why would he lie?"

Ms. Shiphole and Dr. Beamons aren't the only ones who believe in the mystery of the fry. Cryptologist Flank Pegorson has also questioned the veracity of certain fast-food chains' claim over being the original inventor of fry sauce.

"A lot of fools believe that the red, brown, and yellow colors of the rocks are a result of the presence of oxidized iron," Mr. Pergorson says. "The truth is that the colors come from ancient attempts to combine tomato paste with an emulsion of oil, egg yolk, and vinegar... or as the layman calls it: fry sauce."

Could this be true? Had Pergorson and Beamons cracked the code of the unknown?

"Almost undoubtedly," Ms. Shiphole suggests.

If this is true, why was the secret of fry sauce hidden from the world for so long?

Across the pond, archaeologist Herb Georgebet, 7th Earl of Scabthereon, challenged the idea that fry sauce was just confined to the Utah area.

"Whilst many believe that chip sauce was conceived in mountains of Ew-tah, there have been some extwaordinary findings throughout Ew-rope." Lord Georgebet wrote. "As it turns out, Benedictine monks were twusted with the secwets of this dewicious combination, over the space of 200 years."

Early records show that fry sauce, or as it was recorded in ancient scrolls, "cerritulus liquamine oleo lita", was a staple of early Catholic saints. The book of Abbo of Fleury mentions a "frothy delicacy to be placed only upon the palate." Adalbert of Prague was known to have kept a vial hidden inside his hymnal. In fact, recent findings seem to connect fry sauce to the Knights of the First Crusade.

"Wecently we discovered a massive cewemonial hall under a cwusader castle in Northern Iswael," Lord Georgebet continued. "Unearthed in our findings was a massive hidden sepulcher containing a skeweton of Jeffowee De Chawming. He was entombed with many welics, incwuding large pots of wiquid that smewwed of mayonnaises."

Unfortunately, further studies of fry sauce's ancient history were lost when Lord Georgebet died in 1809 following complications from a giraffe bite. Shortly after his death, speculation surrounded the Georgebet aristocracy as being "cursed by the chip."

The last remaining member of the Georgebet aristocracy, a young chav who goes by the name of "Stanks," has turned his back entirely on fry sauce foundations.

"Oi init bruvv. Got my four by four ravers and bass line skankers init sket. We goin' to blow this place out wicked blud." Stanks says.

However, when pressed about any of his great-great-great-great Step-Uncle's findings, Stank is less than cooperative. "Ahhh mate, that's well, dog has it blud. Hush your gums. Oi, let's sketchit yo ay and hit the legs. This is well waffle munter bruv."

Waffle munter, indeed.

The next obvious step in the search for fry sauce history is the Jeffowee De Chawming Museum in Northern France.

"Before we begin," Museum curator Steven Odenthal (not related) began, "The name is pronounced Jeff-oh-ree Day Charming. Georgebet was known to write in rhotacism. Consequently, Georgebet is pronounced Wink Dam Slam Winkle."

The museum holds various De Chawming's… er … De Charmings antiquities, ranging anywhere from saintly bone fragments to the first Howdy Doody candy dispenser.

"Our prize possessions are the pots of the Immaculate Dribbling Cathedral, which are discussed in Georgebet's writings," Odenthal says. "Once a year, our museum offers a smelling festivity wherein the pot's sealings are opened, and all interested parties may take a three-second whiff of the delicacy that was once stored in them."

The festivity, known as the "Come Smell Our Pot" festival, was known to bring chefs worldwide to breathe in the faint aroma. The Chinese philosopher, Xun Kuang, was known to meditate in the smelling room. Renoir, Van Gogh, and even Andy Warhol paid visits to acquire inspiration from the succulent scent.

"Now, we mostly get hippies and burn-outs," Odenthal explains. "I'm guessing it has to do with the name. Regardless, one of those chefs who dealt it and then smelt it was Raynaud Polar."

This revelation somewhat completes the fry sauce circle. In 1924, "Ray" Polar, along with his friend, Juan Carlos Anderson, opened a restaurant together in Salt Lake City. Polar signed over his name and rights and moved to Iowa to begin his life as a quaker, leaving Juan Carlos to run the newly opened diner: Polar Oval. Polar Oval's claim to fame? Fry sauce.

Current CEO and Juan Carlos's grandson, Frank Anderson, seems unsure about the correlation.

"I'm not sure about the whole European involvement with our fry sauce," Anderson states. "Grandpa told me he was carrying bowls of ketchup and mayo to the back, slipped, and the bowls crashed together. Well, as you can imagine, there was sauce everywhere, and consequently, a bit of the mixture fell right onto a side of fries. Grandpa was so embarrassed, he just served the fries to our customers, and the next thing you know... we had a hit on our hands."

At the time of this writing, there are seven statues/areas devoted to fry sauce. Three of them are located within the first Polar Oval diner. Three more are scattered throughout Utah. There is the famous "Fry Sauce Arch" in Southern Utah, the less than famous "Fry Sauce Jetty" in Northern Utah, and the relatively unknown "Fry Sauce Field" in the Santaquin area.

The last known statue greets you as you enter the Jefforee De Charming Museum. It is a bust of De Charming made entirely out of jade and opal. The eyes are 18-carat diamonds and are known to follow you around the room.

"I like to think that De Charming's ghost is in that bust," Odenthal states. "And he's looking at you, smiling, knowing that you are thinking about the wonderful aroma of his pots, and then out of jealousy, he is planning on haunting you until you die."

Odenthal smiles. "But maybe that's just me."

Whether it was born in the canyonlands of Southern Utah, discovered by Monks in some weird area of Europe, or it's the product of a fortunate slip in the kitchen of a Salt Lake City diner, make no mistake: fry sauce is well-loved in every corner of this world.

"Every corner, because the earth is flat," Dr. Beamons states again.

---

Editor's Note: Fry sauce recipes do vary, and some optional ingredients may have been at play during this research.

# Fortune Favors the Bold

## *Tim Keller*

Twice every month, a motley crew of writers descends upon Angie's restaurant in Logan, Utah, ostensibly for dinner and pie. It is here we discuss all things writing-related. Everything from grammar rules to who got their feelers hurt in our critique meeting, to the various merits of literary vs. genre writing styles— That's the first ten minutes anyway.

The following two hours makes for a veritable buffet of topics. At one end of the fifteen-person table, the subject may be gardening, politics, or fishing. In contrast, Downton Abbey might occupy those seated at the other end.

There are, however, a few topics that occasionally capture the interest of everyone. Many of societies' most vexing issues have been aired, and some of the favorites will invariably be brought up if only briefly, every week. Some of these are of a sensitive nature and far too secretive to air here. Others, like, "Should a Galaxy Class Starship engage an Executor Class Star Destroyer, which would win?" Seem to get brought up a lot. As an avowed fan of Star Trek and Star Wars, I have to say I could and have gone on for volumes, but will, out of respect for my audience, and the Angie's fallen— refrain.

It is enough to know that at some point, twice a month, caffeine and carbs will overrule most adult sensibility, and the afore-mentioned, or some other, equally important topic, will be vigorously discussed. Kung Fu vampires, the various problems with the Twilight saga, reasons for the all but universal hatred of Olaf the snowman from Frozen, and BB8 from Star Wars are among the favorites.

Anecdotes also factor heavily. Old favorites are repeated for the sake of newbies, and others, like the one I've been tasked to relate here, are the result of one silly conversation building to another. If the anecdote is good or outrageous enough, the gauntlet will fall, and the raconteur, in this case, me— will be challenged to write and share the piece.

\*

So… once upon a time, several college friends and I welcomed a newbie into our cadre. The freshman in question, being an exceptional young man, possessed of enviable intellect and razor-sharp wit, turned out to be a great fit. But we noticed as time went on that every time we dined out, he would order the meagerest of menu items, eat like a bird and carefully wrap the remaining portion to take home.

A touch of probing found that the boy, having come out too soon, was given a choice, either stay at home and get therapy, or his parents would withdraw all funding for his upcoming education. In an act of stellar courage, he packed what he could carry and, with his life savings from a fast-food summer job, managed to pay for his first semester, a dorm room, and no meal plan.

We took action at once, working out a schedule that ensured at least one of us would take him to eat every day. Owing to its reasonable pricing and enormous portions, The Old Bull was chosen at least a couple times a week.

Having only a passing familiarity with the place, I had yet to understand some of the more idiosyncratic aspects of the authentic cuisine. Everything is made from scratch and will therefore come out a little different every time.

Take the salsa, for instance. While always excellent, it will sometimes be quite mild and others, will be capable of melting through the faux-lava stone bowls. This likely presents no problem for dainty-dippers.

On the other hand, I am a devout super-scooper, especially when the salsa is this good. I could hardly help myself from taking a double portion of the stuff with each chip, almost as if the chip were a mere vehicle for delivering the precious condiment.

One evening, after a particularly potent meal, I felt the urge to "freshen up" as we rose to leave, but the restaurant had a gap in their bathroom stall big enough to watch a movie through. I engaged in some admittedly hasty introspection, weighed all the factors, and decided to wait.

As I dropped our young padawan at his dorm, the mildest of stirrings, no more than an inkling really, again, made itself known. The only real option at that point, however, was a Mos Eisley-style quickie mart or the embarrassment of asking to defile our intrepid young scholar's facilities. I made for home.

As the lights of civilization faded in my rearview mirror, my inkling morphed without warning into what can only be described as contractions—long and severe enough to fold steel. It took several long moments of Lamaze inspired hee hee hoo's to regain my composure.

I hastily considered my options. It was 10 minutes back to civilization to which I could add another ten to find a suitable facility,—or 20 home.

I can make it, I thought, though I sped up just to be sure. No sooner had the needle crept past 70 however, was I gripped with another even more devastating wave — contractions yes, but now Alien in nature. I'm both saddened and relieved Sigourney Weaver was not along for the ride.

Regardless, whether exploding from my abdomen or the only slightly more civilized standard means, this thing was coming out!

A race then, I thought, giving the accelerator a good kick. Beads of sweat formed on my brow as I realized with mounting horror that whatever was in there had reached the end of its journey, and, like Grond at the gates of Gondor, was even now battering against the gate.

I clenched my butt cheeks tightly enough to crush adamantium. Even so, a tiny jet of pressurized gas broke containment and whistled through like high tea. Though it hardly seems possible, I could swear a green mist filled the cabin.

To say my eyes began to water does not do my tear ducts justice.

In desperation, I crossed my legs to help reinforce the clenched sphincter.

The pressure and pain were so intense I actually considered surrender until I saw a divine sign on the side of the road.

"Up ahead, A Texaco! Star of the American road!"

I deftly swing the Caddy into the sort of sideways parking maneuver usually reserved for police chase climaxes, and Bo and Luke Duke, leaped from the car and began moving with all haste for a man resembling a speed walker, with unnaturally erect posture and clenched buttocks that is—toward the restrooms.

Buckets of sweat spewed from every pore. To my great dismay, as I reached the bathroom door, my panic level rose to a stratospheric level.

The door was locked.

I grasped the corner of the building for support as I crossed my legs and waited interminable moments for the room to become available. It was at this point my head must have hit the door because from the other side came a gruff, though relaxed and not entirely unfriendly:

"Occupado"

I used virtually my last ounce of self-control to modulate a semi-nonchalant: "could you hurry please."

"Keep yer pants on buddy! I'll be out in-a-minute,"

A quick look around confirmed I was the subject of many a curious glance. Great, now I could look forward to losing it in front of an audience.

Not that the resulting explosion wouldn't kill every last gawker.

Then, even as my sphincter began to give way—providence stepped in, and the wave passed.

Decision time: "keep my pants on" for Senor Occupado, and hope he'd be finished soon, or make a run for it—really make those last ten minutes count.

I mean, fortune favors the bold… right?

Rocks flew from the wheels of my trusty steed as I raced from the parking lot. No substitute for cubic inches … down Franklin hill and barreling up toward Whitney at over 100 miles per hour, it hit again, this time it felt like half my guts had broken away, and I knew… win or lose, this wave would be the last.

That's when the passenger rear tire blew.

# My Thoughts on Death

## *Spur Nutcheck*

**My Thoughts on Death**

*I've known death for years, and people will ask*
*"Is he as great as we hear?"*
*He's in every war, in most major events*
*Well, let me be perfectly clear:*

*Death is a jerk and he thinks he's so cool*
*Wearing black robes, acting so tough*
*He has a big sickle that he carries around*
*I mean, where does he even get that stuff?*

*He won't ever shut up about how he can fly*
*And that his new ride is a skeleton horse*
*And the ladies all love him, they can't get enough*
*Because in the end - literally - he gets them, of course*

*He knows everyone famous, they're all his friends*
*Does lunch with them all every week*
*Marilyn, Elvis, Gandhi, James Dean*
*At every large gathering, they want him to speak.*

*The truth of it all is he's nothing that great*
*Just a dumb skeleton wrapped in a cloak*
*But don't ever mock him when he comes around*
*Because on your words, you will choke.*

# Life Is Beautiful

## *Spur Nutcheck*

### Life Is Beautiful

*I wake up each morning to the beautiful sun*
*Basking in its eternal warm graces*
*I stare off my porch at this wonderful land*
*Punch dumb frogs in their faces*

*America, the land of the free*
*Each day I am agog*
*Purple mountains, spacious skies*
*Let's all go punch a frog*

*No poetry can emulate*
*A lonely dusty road*
*A clear blue sky or rainy day*
*Make sure you're not punching a toad*

*And each night I feel a lovely breeze*
*That leaves me feeling lucid*
*Could this be what Heaven feels like?*
*99 percent of frogs are stupid*

*The sounds of lovebirds in the sky*
*Their singsongs in the switch*
*I whistle with them, soft but strong*
*Kick every frog into a ditch*

## Jon Baty

*When I'm laying by a campfire*
*And all the stars take up their places*
*One star shoots across, my thoughts are lost*
*Every frog I know is racist*

*It's hard to sum up my incredible life*
*And express every emotion*
*I think back on the best of times*
*Like throwing frogs into the ocean*

*When I meet people here and there*
*I share my beautiful life*
*But then I quickly change the subject*
*To when a frog stole my second wife*

# The Dog Who Loved Me

## *Spur Nutcheck*

**The Dog Who Loved Me**
One night as I got up to pee
My dog just sat and stared at me
He cocked his head, squinted his eyes
That's when I knew, my dog's a spy

It came to me, right then and there
That traitor follows me everywhere
His brain making the mental notes
"I'll fix him one day," I'm sure he gloats

He's seen me in my low of lows
Scratchin' my butt; pickin' my nose
This dog I thought that I could trust
My face covered in Cheeto dust

Then suddenly I started thinking
Was it poison I was drinking?
Could I trust him? Maybe he
Was a member of the KGB?

And then I chuckled, turned and said
There's no way this dog wants me dead
I give him shelter here and food
His life with me is far too good

But then he shot me in the thigh
I fell down hard, whilst screaming why?
What kind of monster could do that?
Took off his mask... he was a cat.

# Birthing Hips and the Santa Clause

## *Steve Odenthal*

We take things for granted in life—little things and big things, quiet pleasures, and outright gifts that we assume will always be there. Sometimes we appreciate those things, whether they are materially tangible or a deep emotional attachment when we have them daily in our lives. Still, most of the time, we only become fully aware of the significance of our treasured gift when it is gone. I have always thought of filling voids and giving freely to others as part of my earthly contract. I try to invoke what I call the Santa Clause regularly.

The image of a Santa in my life delighted me as a child and delivered to me the extraordinary gift of giving to others. Circumstances were such that the Santa my siblings and I knew was one who gave freely to others whose conditions were a bit more wanting than ours but still had time to stop by after we slept to check in on us and partake of a cookie and milk break during his yearly trek. As we clung to the mystique of it all, a part of each of us yearned a bit more each year to fill the red suit and bring others the happiness of the season. Once our childhood haze had receded, family members assumed a helper role in providing the awe of the season for others. The Santa Clause kicked-in and we were all the better for it.

As an adult, I have had the opportunity to bring my children up in a world where the Santa Clause is still in vogue. It is just a little harder to spot unless I look for it. But it is there. People who go out of their way to give to others without a thought of repayment or service in return, they qualify as Santa Clausers. You can find these people too. They are everywhere and in all walks of life, laboring and using their talents to others' benefit. Sometimes it just takes a moment before we recognize what they are doing, but they are there.

One of the Santa Clausers in my life was Dee Pace, an actor of some re-noun in and around Northern Utah. As luck would have it, I was able to share a bit of the stage with him as he played the role of Kris Kringle in *Miracle on 34th Street* at the Heritage Theatre in our area. Dee's presence in a cast ensured a full house of eager patrons who knew they would get their money's worth with any role that Dee took on. While Dee loved performing and people, that love was quickly matched by castmates and audiences alike, each adoring his caring and pleasant personality. I will admit that I got involved with the Christmas show due to seeing an opportunity to work creatively with Dee. Sure, some will say that my wife, an assistant director, might have had a bit to do with my involvement, but the chance to be in a cast with Dee was the real clincher. I had put an entry on my bucket list many years ago, after seeing Pace captivate the audience in a regional theatre production of *A Funny Thing Happened on the Way to the Forum*, to somehow work with this talented man. I was reviewing the Forum show and gave it a huge and well-deserved accolade for my local publication. At that time, I figured that perhaps I would one-day write a role for him in one of my stage plays. And I did. He just never knew about it.

The seasoned director of *Miracle on 34th Street* was well-aware of Dee's strong singing and dancing abilities and quickly came to grips with my talents on-stage, which might best be described in this way, "Steve sings and dances as well as most shrubbery." Her challenge in this production, filled with top-notch performers, was to place me in the best position to counterbalance the talent without harming the scene. She did a beautiful job, so I am told, and the show performed to sell-out audiences. Many of my friends still talk about that Christmas run and express surprise when I mention that I not only remember the show but was in it. See, the director did a great job, and the entire cast was tremendous.

For me, the show had several highlights on-stage, but most treasured to me are the short conversations that I engaged in with Dee in and after rehearsals and performances. I got the chance to ask questions about his career in acting, what roles he most enjoyed, what most mattered to him in life, friends we had in common, and I even mentioned that I had a role written for him in a play I had penned. Conversation with this man was always comfortable and open, but as I look back now, I did feel just a touch of urgency to gather his insights. I have learned since then that many others shared that feeling; one friend in common told me, "I always felt that I was one of Dee's closest friends. But he made everyone feel that way." I agree with that sentiment. Dee was genuine and kind to everyone, which suited him well in his years as a teacher and administrator. See, I told you he was a Santa Clauser.

Many of my great memories of that show involve Dee and his ability to ply his craft while always looking out for other cast members. Whether it was a friendly greeting that stretched into a short conversation with a new young actor, or a word of encouragement to an oldster (me) putting the choreographer through her paces with both left feet—sorry, Sandy, giving his best was the norm for this actor.

The memory that sticks with me the most from our performances occurred in the third show of our seventeen-performance run. At one point, Kris Kringle appears in the Macy's store, and the shoppers gather excitedly at his feet as he starts one of the main numbers in the show. In my ensemble role of a shopper with young grand-daughter in tow, our blocking was to hurry down-center to plop down at Kris(Dee's) feet while he sang out to the audience and broadly gestured in a Kringley way. I had no problem with this blocking, and I must admit that I was thankful that the original idea had changed a bit, allowing me to take a granddaughter with me. It had always seemed a little bit of special to hustle downstage as a 60-year-old man by myself only to collapse at the feet of and hero-worship the jolly old elf. Yes, it worked much better with a grandchild accompanying me, but the timing was crucial for us to get in place before Dee made his grand gesture and held his note. We needed to be down and out of sightline for the full Santa effect, and in the first two shows, we made it look easy. My stage granddaughter had the flexibility and grace to glide into position and perfectly alight on the floor throughout the run of the show. Show number three was my Waterloo.

As I moved down and center, all seemed in order, but when I lowered into position, a loud "POP" rang out, and I toppled the last third of the trip to the floor. There was no accompanying pain, and I did keep in character, so that was good—my immediate thought was maybe it was just thunder as no one else seemed to have noticed. Dee made his gesture while holding the extended note. I silently wondered if I was going to be able to jump up and into my next part of the choreography, which was coming soon. Dee finished his note, and while the music continued between verses of his solo, he looked down to me and mouthed "Are you alright? Can you get back up?" The only answer I had was, "We'll see."

I did make it back up to my feet, and no one seemed the wiser, so the show went off without a hitch. In fact, the next fourteen shows ran well. I can't say that there was no pain, but I was smart enough to avoid much medical attention until after our final performance when the diagnosis came that I had torn a small part of my Piriformis muscle. The physical therapist explained that muscle is instrumental in keeping the hips aligned and walking straight, so he advised that I obey all traffic rules and avoid both Highway Patrolmen and field sobriety tests. Oh yes, and that there would be pain—quite a bit and for quite a while. He gave one last word of warning: I would never have perfect birthing hips again.

For his part, Dee knew that I had injured myself, and he was quite concerned after the show. Ever the veteran of the stage, he even told me what had occurred to him as to how to get me assistance while keeping the scene intact. He was a pro. I will always remember the honor it was to be in that cast. You see that show was the final performance run for Dee Pace, the man who entertained and enriched the lives of thousands as he chose to take on a service mission for his church. Service, and specifically that calling, was one that he looked forward to as a chance to serve with his loving wife, Nedra, and to serve his fellow man.

And they did serve well in what all of us back home expected to be a two-year calling; the couple toiled lovingly far away from their home in Box Elder County. The year 2020 was still in its infancy when we heard the terrible news that Dee picked up COVID-19, the deadly Coronavirus spreading across the globe. After a long and courageous struggle that ended in a hospital in Green Bay, Wisconsin, my community's friend, mentor, and role model passed from this earth. His doctors and medical staff, working unbelievably long hours and fighting a fight that no one had answers to, never caught a glimpse of the larger than life, wonderful person they had in their care. They never got to see him on stage or the many characters he made his own. The hospital never knew the lengths to which Dee Pace would go and the sacrifices he would make to contribute to building a better world. Those physicians and nurses would never hear their patient's gentle voice or experience his quick wit. All those front-line heroes could do was their very best in a tragic time. But Dee, husband, father, grandfather, and friend to all, became the first actively serving missionary of his church to fall to this pandemic illness.

In the wake of this plague upon us, many families are dealing with voids where loved ones once were. My heart reaches out to each of them. I think about the loss of Dee Pace a lot and remember that I was so excited to share the story of my now funny walk with him. I think he would have had a good laugh with me about it. I was writing it up when we got word, as I was writing a book of humor at that time. I had to stop. It was a much different story than this one. But this one is more appropriate for the time when we still are in the throes of this deadly virus. We do the best we can, and we invoke the Santa Clause to make a dreary world brighter by giving to others the absolute best of ourselves. That is what Dee would do and always did. We miss you, Dee.

# Afterword

The year 2020 has been unlike any year that we have experienced in our lifetimes. Many hills and obstacles have presented themselves to each of us, from political unrest to a worldwide pandemic. I hope that you have enjoyed a short time away from all that while reading these pages. Humor is a wonderful thing, and it serves to soothe our souls in troubling times when done right. The writers included in this anthology have purposefully written about simple things, everyday life events that could have happened to anyone of us. Each one of the humorists faced the same large looming dark clouds which monopolized the year 2020, but through their imagination and gift with words, they managed to bring a memory, a smile, and optimism to you, the reader. At least, that was our goal. I hope that you achieved all three. Be safe and look forward, my friends.

# Appendix

# About Our Humorists

It is my honor to introduce these writers to you. Mixed in this anthology are some of the best humor voices, having roots in Utah that you will find. Together they tell a Special Blend of stories at a time when we all need to laugh. Each story, bit of prose, or poem was selected in a time when the world around us is changing in ways no one could have predicted. Some of the writing is sure to make you laugh out loud, other pieces will bring a smile and a more profound thought or two, but all the work here is worthy of praise. I think you will enjoy the break from reality that you will find here. Let me tell you a bit about my friends…

**Jon Baty** – I first met Jon after an Improv show that destroyed the audience. He made a big impression on me, and then we found that he hailed from the same area where I currently live. I have followed his career for several years and count him as a true friend, so it was a must that I ask him to contribute to this book. His alter-ego Spur Nutcheck knocks me out, and I understand that there are some behind the scenes negotiations for an OdieGroup Press-Spur Nutcheck collaboration in the future.

**Alice M Batzel** – Alice has graced the pages of two OdieGroup Press anthologies now. She tells a story in a gentle way rich in southern charm, as her roots are in Florida. Alice has found life in Utah pleasurable, but her memories of warm sun and toes covered with beach sand are never too far from her mind. She is a veteran writer with more than a few fans, including me. You will enjoy her soft touch with humor.

**James D Beers** – James is a good friend and writer of many humor stories. He and I immediately bonded over our love of the great humor of Patrick McManus, and you will notice a similar tone when you fall into his work. James brings a couple of pieces to this anthology, one of which touches on the human condition's fragility in this time of pandemic while showing that humor is vital. It is an essential contribution to this collection. His roots are stretching a little as he transplanted his family to a new job in Arkansas, but he will always be in love with the Intermountain West.

**Monique Berish** – Monique is a Facebook friend who I found in the League of Utah Writers. Her voice is outstanding. Her quick wit is on display regularly on Social Media, and I can't tell you how many times I have mentioned her wit to friends. She tells us of being a transplant to Utah and her Yoga life in two hilarious stories. I think you will find her a hard act to follow but read on in the book as we have plenty more you will enjoy.

**Richard Crawford** – Richard slipped quietly into our Brigham City Writers group meeting one evening when we had adjusted our location to a condominium clubhouse for that night because our usual meeting place was closed. He earned the group's respect during the critiques by adding a comment or two. At the end of the meeting, we talked, and I found out that Richard had stumbled upon us accidentally. He thought the meeting was for and about empty nesters but had a good enough time that he decided to stay. His contribution is his first published story. He did alright.

**Eric R Jensen** – My friend, Eric Jensen, is one of the funniest people I have ever met. More than that, he is a gift to the Utah theater scene. I had to ask him to contribute to this effort, and despite the brevity of his funny but tender story, his talent shines brightly through. If I am a little down, any project Eric is involved in is the first place I will look for a pick-me-up. I'm proud to call Eric and his family (Sandy and Austinn) friends. If you find yourself in Salt Lake City, reward yourself with the Off-Broadway Theatre or their Improv group "Laughing Stock."

**Tim Keller** – Not too far away from Brigham City, where I hang out, is a sleepy little valley and a town called Logan. There must be something in the water up there because Tim is part of a writers group that boasts many award-winning writers. Tim has been at the forefront of that group for several years, and I can attest that he teaches a pretty, pretty good humor class at writer conferences in the

Intermountain West. The three stories that he contributed are slices of life that you don't read just anywhere. You might find one to follow with Tim Keller.

**DeAnne Mattix** – DeAnne is a delight to know. She and I have been friends for several years while paying our dues in the Brigham City Writers group. She writes in several genres, but her natural humor comes through loud and clear in the two stories she contributed. Relatable and funny, DeAnne Mattix is an author you will want to follow.

**Don Miles** – I met Don when I was teaching a "writing with humor" class at the 2019 LDSPMA annual conference. I sized up my audience, as you do, and immediately caught sight on the back row of a scowling figure who had a pen and paper out and was ready to go. Somehow, his countenance had me doubting that *I* was "ready to go." I spoke with him after class, and after listening to a few of his stories, I knew I had to invite him to participate in this anthology. It was a strong feeling—but I didn't choose to press my luck and ask him if he got anything out of the class. I think you will enjoy what he brings to the table here.

**Mike Nelson** – Mike and I go way back. At least we are in the same age group, and people our age all go way back. Last year Mike contributed to our first anthology of humor based in Utah, and he came back for more. He loves the outdoors, and his steps into humor writing have been fun to watch. I think that Mike's other genres may also interest you, but he has a funny side, which I do enjoy.

**Tyler Brian Nelson** – Tyler is also a veteran of the anthologies, having penned a piece for our *Heard at a Utah Diner* collection. He is still at the beginning of his writing career, but it is one that you will want to track because he will become quite successful. Remember, you found him here first. You will enjoy his storytelling.

**Steve Odenthal** – I've known this guy all of my life. Still not too impressed, but he assures me he will do better. He likes to write slices of life, taking train-wreck experiences, and humorously re-spinning them. He has set a goal to put out a book of collected humor (anthology) each year, hoping to expose some great humorists along the way. His hope with this collection is that the reader can find a smile and perhaps tie it into a memory that brings a warm feeling at a time when light and warmth are desperately needed.

# Jon Baty

Hailing from a small Northern Utah shanty town, Jon Baty was nominated by his high school peers as "Class Idiot" (true) and immediately left that area as soon as he could (very true). Following dreams of writing, he regrettably graduated with a degree in Public Relations and the relatable subject of World Literature. Following this, his Dad said to him, "at least you left college well-read."

He has been fortunate enough to display his talents in a wide variety of things. You may have seen him in film, on the stage, in commercials, performing comedy across the nation, and/or fronting various 'nearly famous' bands. Having a lot of great moments in his career, one of his fondest was when the actor Robert Forster told him he was "incredibly *cussing* funny."

Currently, he resides in the Salt Lake City area with his beautiful wife, two amazing daughters (one of them has yet to be seen, but will make her appearance soon), and a very anxiety ridden Snorkie. He also fancies himself a pop artist and sells his paintings under the name, "JB Draws the Hits". More information can be found at:

https://www.facebook.com/drawthehits/

Thank you to Steve and the OdieGroup Press for allowing me to rant.

# Alice M Batzel

Alice M Batzel is a published author, playwright, journalist, poet, and freelance writer. She's a displaced "beach writer" at heart, having been raised on the NW Florida Gulf Coast, although she considers herself fortunate to call northern Utah "home" for the past 40 years. Alice and her husband reside in the rural community of Brigham City at the foot of the majestic Wasatch Mountains. Rural living provides much observation of family life, and humor runs pretty thick here. Every day you don't have to look far to find a smile, a chuckle, and a laugh. And then there are those knee-slapping gut-busting laughs that take over you when you least expect it, whether it's from something you've observed or something you've experienced. Laughter truly is the good medicine of life, and we're all in need of a daily dose of it! Life in Utah gives you a reason to laugh, and you're grateful for it! Idle Isle Café, Maddox Ranch House, and Peach City Drive-in are some of her favorite local dining establishments where she enjoys good food, laughter, and making memories with family and friends.

**www.alicembatzel.com**

# James D Beers

James D. Beers is an award-winning humorist and a life-long ice cream aficionado raised in the wilds of Northern Idaho and presently living in Central Arkansas with his wife Jenna and son Joseph. He loves cheese, chocolate, steak (not necessarily in that order, but ice cream is always first), and driving questionable two-track roads in the wilderness. Occasionally he picks up a fly rod or spinning reel to try his luck at trout and monster Bluegill. Since his twelfth birthday, he's worn out oodles of hiking boots in search of the elusive whitetail deer and Rocky Mountain elk of the American West and, most recently, the wily turkey of the Southern hardwoods.

When he's not busy laughing over a humorous story draft, James also pens ghost stories and middle-grade adventures. He's been involved with several writing conferences, including as a committee member with the League of Utah Writers, the World Horror Convention 2016, and the Utah Book Marketing Conference. You can read his work in A Knack for Embarrassment (2016), Weird Wasatch (2018), Laughs & Spooks, Volume 1 (2018), At First Glance (2018), Heard at a Utah Diner (2019), Within Earshot: Rumors, Whispers, and Lies (2020), and Heard at a Utah Diner, Volume 2 (forthcoming) - all of which are available on several online retailers including Amazon.

writingwithbeers.com

# Monique Berish

Monique Berish is a Board Certified Psychiatric nurse with more than 20 years of experience. From the rough streets of Perth Amboy, New Jersey, to the wilds of Alaska, Monique wandered through much of the United States, gleaning experience from her adventures along the way. Raised by a schizophrenic father and a clinically depressed mother, she managed to forge her path into healing and kindled a passion for caring for the mentally ill. In addition to memoir, she writes articles on various mental health topics, consults as a psychiatric and mental health expert for publications, and publishes humor-based short stories.

https://moniqueberish.com

# Don Miles

Don Miles is a senior editor in the Publishing Services Department for The Church of Jesus Christ of Latter-day Saints. He has worked there for over 30 years. He has also worked as a farmer, Santa Claus, and construction worker, and he taught writing and other courses at BYU, UVCC, and the University of Phoenix for 20 years. He has a B.A. and M.A. in English from BYU. He received the graduate student instructor award from BYU and the distinguished teaching award from the University of Phoenix. He received a scholarship from the Outdoor Writer's Association of America. He has published 2 books and about 120 articles. He and his wife Kristi have 6 sons and 11 grandchildren. He enjoys backpacking, camping, hunting, shooting, and watching grandchildren. He braids bullwhips and other leather projects.

# Mike Nelson

Mike graduated from Weber State University with a degree in Accounting. He is the proud father of six children, an active member of his church, and currently lives with his wife of fifty-one years in Northern Utah. He served in the United States Airforce in Communications Intelligence and was stationed near Istanbul, Turkey, for thirty-eight months before his honorable discharge in 1974. He is currently an active member of the League of Utah Writers.

Although he has been writing most of his life, he didn't get serious until he retired from ATK in 2014. His third novel, "Clairvoyant," was awarded the Utah League of Writer's Silver Quill award for adult literature in 2019. His novel, "Clairvoyant Book 2" is his fifth published novel and a sequel to "Clairvoyant." He has published numerous short stories in League anthologies.

Mike loves most things out-of-doors and, in his younger days, backpacked, hunted, and fished the mountains of Idaho, Utah, and Wyoming. Now that he has hung up his hiking boots and backpack, he still enjoys the great out-of-doors with his wife from the seat of his side-by-side. He is seen from time-to-time fishing the waters of Southern Idaho from his pontoon boat.

# Tyler Brian Nelson

Tyler Nelson is an avid short-story writer and aspiring novelist whose work and literary interests range from the Dr. Suess-esque to the minute realism and historical fiction of Leo Tolstoy. His work can be found in Volume 1 of the Utah Humor Anthology, and in the Owl Canyon Press Hackathon winners anthology, *Where the Ride Ends*. Tyler enjoys hiking, basketball, playing the guitar, traveling with his wife, and seldom leaves home without a good book. You can follow his literary progress and even give feedback at

https://wordpress.com/people/team/tybnelson.home.blog

# Steve Odenthal

Steve Odenthal calls Utah his home and talks about that state frequently. Most of the time, his remarks are printable, but both he and his long-suffering wife, Valerie, take pride in finding glimpses and voices of humor here. This collection of humor is part of an annual search that brings new and older voices out onto the page for your enjoyment.

The first book in his pet Utah Humor Anthology Project was released in 2019, *Heard at a Utah Diner* has acquired a nice following, and we are hoping for the same success with this volume.

Steve released a collection of his own humor in May 2020, Chimney Fishing Tales, which taught him his first lesson of writing comedy during a pandemic. Ever a slow-learner or just stubborn, he believes that we all need to laugh sometimes. Now would be good.

Follow Steve on Facebook, Twitter, and Instagram.

# Invitation to BardZi Reviews

Have you heard about BardZi.com? Probably not. Yet. But you will soon. You see, this book is one of the very first to participate in the BardZi.com site. We hope it becomes a site you grow to love, and we look forward to your active participation in it.

What is BardZi? It is a social site that brings avid readers and exciting new writers together in one place. You see, for years, authors have worked hard to gain exposure for their books in areas where avid readers (like you) could find them. That is not as easy as it sounds. Sure shelf space is plentiful at places like Amazon, online, Barnes & Noble, as well as in thousands of independent bookstores across the country, but those places are not always where the right and loyal readers dwell. Authors and readers often run on entirely different treadmills, and it has been too easy to miss each other. We want to close that gap.

Visit BardZi.com to leave a review on this and other books that you love. Doing so gets you one step closer to your favorite authors and, even better, lets you mingle among other avid readers in your genre. It's free for the reader and a great way to get involved. You will find insights from authors and other readers' recommendations for your next great read. Check us out today at BardZi.com